Intra Muros Cuncti Inter Se

D0363954

THE HOME UNIVERSITY LIBRARY
OF MODERN KNOWLEDGE

96

POLITICAL THOUGHT IN ENGLAND

BACON TO HALIFAX

Political Thought in England

BACON TO HALIFAX

G. P. GOOCH
C.H., D.Litt., F.B.A.

LONDON
OXFORD UNIVERSITY PRESS
NEW YORK TORONTO

Oxford University Press, Amen House, London E.C.4

GLASGOW NEW YORK TORONTO MELBOURNE WELLINGTON
BOMBAY CALCUTTA MADRAS KARACHI KUALA LUMPUR
CAPE TOWN IBADAN NAIROBI ACCRA

First edition 1915
Reprinted 1923, 1926, 1927, 1929,
1933 *and* 1944
Reset in 1946 *and reprinted in* 1950, 1955 *and* 1960

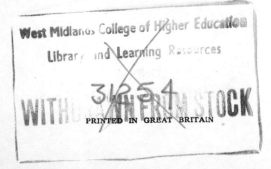
PRINTED IN GREAT BRITAIN

CONTENTS

CHAPTER I

JAMES I, BACON, AND THE DIVINE RIGHT OF KINGS

I

IF the sixteenth century was the era of theological controversy, the seventeenth was above all the age of political discussion. The Reformation had broken the traditional European system in pieces, and it was necessary to erect some other structure under the shelter of which men and nations could live in safety. Such shelter was found in the increase of the authority of the temporal ruler; but the exorbitant claims of kings led by an inevitable reaction to the demand for popular rights. If the absolute State was the child and heir of the Reformation, democracy was its residuary legatee. Thinkers from Bacon to Locke, statesmen from James I to Halifax, devoted themselves to working out a new basis for human association in place of the feudal and ecclesiastical principles which had disappeared for ever. Here is the key to the political thought of the seventeenth century.

The power that was lost by the Papacy and the Church was grasped by Henry VIII and held firmly in his strong hands; and in the struggle for national existence which filled the reign of Elizabeth the country was content that its destinies should be controlled by a powerful and popular monarch. 'Nothing, no worldly thing under the sun', she declared, 'is so dear to me as the love and goodwill of my subjects'; and her people knew that she was speaking the truth. The nation consented to the Tudor despotism; but it was only as champions of the national aspirations, religious and political, that the Tudors were able to exercise an autocratic sway. With the defeat of the Armada the country began to realize that the need for an iron hand had passed, and when the virgin Queen was in her grave new breezes began to blow. Devotion to her had been personal, not official. The individualistic leaven of the Reformation had been silently at work for two generations, and the Puritan sects had convinced themselves that autocracy was incompatible with the religious freedom they claimed for themselves as the highest of earthly privileges. If a conflict was to be avoided between the Crown and the people it could only be by the exercise of unusual tact, and by the recognition that the time was ripe for a cautious advance in the direction of political and ecclesiastical liberty. Largely as a result of Tudor policy political power had passed from the nobles to the country gentry and the mercantile classes. The succession was no longer in danger, and the motives for acquiescence in autocracy had disappeared. A wiser ruler than James might have guided the steps of his people along the paths of progress; but he was utterly lacking in the intuitive perception of popular feeling which saved Elizabeth from irreparable blunders. While a large section of his subjects desired a greater latitude than they had enjoyed or the European situation permitted under Elizabeth, the King entertained a higher notion of his powers and possessed less capacity to rule than his gifted predecessor. While England was rapidly growing up, he determined to treat her as a ward.

The political philosophy of James arose in large measure from the experiences of his early life. The precocious lad had been filled with indignation as he came to realize that the office of King carried with it little power and inspired scant respect. His father had been murdered, his mother chased from the throne. Above all, the Presbyterians scoffed at the secular power, and their leaders audaciously asserted the right of subjects to control and cashier their rulers. It has been truly said that Calvin led the revolt of the Reformation Church against the Reformation State. 'No oath or promise', declared Knox, 'can bind the people to obey and maintain tyrants against God; and if they have ignorantly chosen such as after declare themselves unworthy, most justly may they depose and punish them.' Andrew Melville taught the same doctrine in his lectures at St. Andrews. The young King's tutor, Buchanan, the prince of Humanists, expressed the almost universal conviction of Scotland in his famous treatise, *De Jure Regni*, which declared that a ruler derived his entire authority from the people, and quoted the Scriptural precept that wicked men should be cut off. In France the Huguenots had both preached and practised rebellion. It is not surprising that the observations and humiliations of his early manhood should have crystallized in his pregnant aphorism, 'No Bishop, No King'.

At the age of thirty-two James recorded his political convictions in two treatises of remarkable interest. The earliest, entitled *Basilicon Doron*, was prepared for the guidance of his eldest son Henry, and was not written for publication. The first part, dealing with a king's duty to God, declares that no man is worthy to govern a Christian people who fears and loves not the Divine Majesty. The second, *A King's Duty in His Office*, distinguishes the lawful ruler from the tyrant. The latter feels no responsibility towards God, and his subjects owe him no allegiance. A lawful king, on the other hand, occupies a noble position, and James speaks with passionate indignation of those who refuse to recognize it. 'I was calumniated in their sermons not for any vice in me, but because I was a king. For they told their flocks that kings and princes were naturally enemies to the Church. Take heed, therefore, my son, to such Puritans, very pests in the Church and Commonwealth.' The whole people of Scotland, he added, shared the fault of judging and speaking rashly of their prince. A king should only summon Parliament when new laws were needed, which would be but seldom. He should diligently study the history of his own and other countries, though not, of course, 'such infamous invectives as Buchanan or Knox'. The concluding part of the treatise discusses a king's behaviour in indifferent things. As a king was as one set on a stage, even little matters possessed importance. It was essential to lead a pure life and to be temperate in meat and drink. 'Beware chiefly of drunkenness, which is a beastly vice.' The ruler, again, could not be too careful in his companions and his games, his language and his clothes. The little treatise leaves an agreeable impression of the writer's sincerity. If the maxims embodied rather his ideal than his practice, they made it clear that he possessed as lofty a conception of the duties as of the power of the royal office.

While the *Basilicon Doron* took the form of fatherly advice to a young prince, the *True Law of Free Monarchies or the Mutual Duty betwixt a free King and his Subjects* was a systematic political treatise, addressed to his countrymen. The duty of a prince to his subjects, he declared, was plainly set down in Scripture.

A loving father found his joy in the good of his children. As the head cares for the body, so does the king care for his people. Above the people and above the law, he is subject to God and his conscience alone. 'A good king will frame all his actions according to the law; yet he is not bound thereto but of his good will and for good example to his subjects. He is master over every person, having power over life and death. For though a just prince will not take the life of any of his subjects without a clear law, yet the same laws whereby he taketh them are made by himself or his predecessors.' The kings of Scotland, he declares bluntly, were the authors and makers of laws, not the laws of the kings. They are, however, bound by their coronation oath to preserve religion and the 'good laws' made by their predecessors. The assumption throughout is that kings are wise and good and their subjects weak and ignorant. A king, declared the royal author, was a great schoolmaster for the whole land. A 'Free Monarchy' was a monarchy free to do what it pleased.

James was too well read in history not to know that kings were not always paragons of virtue; but he declines to alter his system. 'The wickedness of the king can never make them that are ordained to be judged by him to become his judges.' In the first place, instead of relieving the State, they would double its distress; for a king can never be so monstrously vicious but that he will not generally favour justice and maintain order. Secondly, a wicked king is sent by God as a plague on people's sins, and it is unlawful to shake off the burden which God has laid upon them. 'Patience, earnest prayer and amendment of their lives are the only lawful means to move God to relieve them of that heavy curse.' The royal publicist then grapples with the argument from the pact between the king and his subjects at his coronation. 'As to this contract I deny it is made, though I confess a king promiseth to discharge truly his office.' But who shall judge whether a breach has taken place? If the people, then they are the judge in their own cause. Clearly God alone can decide. 'He must first give sentence on a king before the people can think themselves freed of their oath.' How God is to convey the signal to the sorely tried people we do not learn. For practical purposes the only check on an evil king is his fear of punishment in the life to come, which is certain to be terrible. 'The further a king is preferred by God above all other degrees of men, the greater is his obligation to his Maker.' Nowhere is the Divine Right of kings—the doctrine, that is, that monarchy is divinely ordained that hereditary right is indefeasable, that kings are accountable to God alone, and that resistance to a lawful king is sin—more concisely formulated or defended with more unfaltering conviction than in the pages of the British Solomon.

Holding such views when merely King of Scotland, it was not likely that the estimate of his powers would be diminished when James found himself ruler of a larger empire, not by statute, nomination or selection, but by right of birth alone. His earliest utterances provoked an 'Apology' from Parliament which clearly revealed its determination to assert its rights, and plainly told the King that he had been misinformed, and that his assertions tended directly 'to the utter overthrow of the very fundamental privileges of our House and therein of the rights and liberties of the whole Commons'. In his speech to Parliament in 1609, reprinted in the stately folio of his works in

1616, the doctrines of the 'True Law of Free Monarchies' were reaffirmed in uncompromising terms. 'Kings are justly called gods; for they exercise a manner of resemblance of Divine power upon earth. For if you will consider the attributes of God, you shall see how they agree in the person of a king. God hath power to create or destroy, make or unmake at His pleasure, to give life or send death, to judge all and to be accountable to none. And the like power have kings. They make and unmake their subjects; they have power of raising up and casting down; of life and death; judges over all their subjects and in all cases, yet accountable to none but God. They have power to exalt low things and abase high things and to make of their subjects like men at chess.' 'The state of monarchy is the supremest thing on earth', he added in 1610; 'for kings are not only God's lieutenants upon earth, but even by God Himself they are called gods.' 'As it is atheism and blasphemy', he declared in a speech in the Star Chamber in 1616, 'to dispute what God can do, so it is presumption and high contempt in a subject to dispute what a king can do or to say that a king cannot do this or that.' In a letter to the Commons in 1621 the King complained that certain fiery and popular spirits had dared to debate and argue publicly on matters far above their reach and capacity. The Speaker was ordered to inform them that 'none should presume to meddle with anything concerning our government or deep matters of State'. When Raleigh appealed to James, in his dialogue on the *Prerogative of Parliaments*, to withdraw his unpopular schemes for raising money and to throw himself on the love of his subjects like Elizabeth, he replied by suppressing the work. Though sympathy with the

Dutch was a national sentiment, James used to maintain that they were rebels engaged in resistance to their lawful king. He even declared that it was unfit for a subject to speak disrespectfully of any anointed king, 'though at hostility with us'. Under the Tudors king and Parliament had been joint organs of the Commonwealth. Here for the first time was absolutism, pure and undefiled. Before this earthly divinity the majesty of the law and the prerogatives of Parliament shrank back rebuked. The realm of England was the slave and plaything of its ruler, and the traditional distinction between British and Continental monarchy disappeared.

These novel and extravagant claims found ready support among the Anglican clergy and in the Universities. While the Puritan sects placed obedience to conscience before obedience to their ruler, the theologians of the State Church proclaimed the divine right of kings and the duty of unconditional obedience to their commands. There is not a trace of the doctrine in Hooker; but the Jacobean divines soon learned their lesson. Indeed, in one important respect they went beyond the King. A collection of canons was drawn up by Convocation in 1606 under the influence of Gunpowder Plot, in which the divine authority even of a *de facto* government was proclaimed. James refused to ratify the canons, pointing out that on these principles should the King of Spain conquer the country his right to the crown would be divine, and no one might try to expel the usurper and restore the lawful ruler. The clergy vied with one another in emphasizing the religious aspect of kingship and the semi-divine character of the King. Expressions such as His Sacred Majesty and Thine Anointed Servant now became common. In a court sermon Sanderson, the favourite chaplain of the King and Regius Professor of Divinity at Oxford, inveighed against taking up arms against a lawful sovereign for any reason whatever; 'not for the maintenance of the lives and liberties of ourselves or others; not for the defence of religion; not, if that could be imagined possible, for the salvation of a soul, no, not for the redemption of the whole world'. The clergy supported the King's prerogative as the most effective weapon in their truceless war against the Papacy on one front and Puritanism on the other. To exalt the Crown was to strengthen the Church.

A dramatic collision between the newly adopted doctrine and public opinion occurred early in the reign of Charles I. In 1626 a divine named Sibthorpe preached on Apostolic Obedience before the judges at Northampton. Rulers, he declared, must be obeyed, 'whether the prince be a believer or an infidel, whether he rule justly or unjustly, courteously or cruelly'. If the prince imposed an immoderate, even an unjust tax, the subject was bound in conscience to submit. 'If princes command anything which subjects may not perform because it is contrary to the laws of God or nature or impossible, subjects are bound to undergo punishment without either resistance or reviling, and so yield a passive obedience where they cannot exhibit an active one.' The King commanded Archbishop Abbot to license the discourse for the Press, and on his refusal placed him in confinement. The sermon was promptly licensed by a more accommodating divine, and its author became a royal chaplain. In the following year a still more unabashed statement of absolutism was made by Mainwaring in a sermon preached before Charles himself. 'Among all the powers ordained of

God the royal is the most high, strong and large. No power in the world or in the Church can lay restraint upon it. That sublime power which resides in earthly potentates is not a derivation or collection of human power but a participation of God's own omnipotency.' To obey kings was an ordinance of God. 'No persons, be they never so great, can be privileged from their power, nor exempted from their care, be they never so mean. The laws take their binding force from the supreme will of their liege lord.' The payment of taxes imposed by the king could not be refused without peril of damnation. 'Though any king should command flatly against the law of God, they must endure with patience whatever penalty his pleasure should inflict upon them who would desire rather to obey God than man.' Even Laud remonstrated against the printing of a discourse which, he declared, would be very distasteful to the people; but the King was resolute, and the sermon appeared. The Commons replied by impeaching Mainwaring, who was condemned to a fine, imprisonment and suspension. Pardoned by his master, he ultimately rose to a bishopric. Despite the resounding rebuke of Parliament, the divinity of kings became in an increasing degree the common faith of the clergy. Even shrewd and witty Fuller declared that none might search the reasons of their actions but such as stood on an equal basis with them, and abruptly closed his discussion of 'the King' with the words, 'But I must stay or fall. My sight fails me, dazzled with the lustre of majesty.'

The doctrine of divine right found no supporter in the Parliaments of the first two Stuarts; yet a number of causes combined to render its prevalence in clerical circles intelligible. The tendency of mankind to invest its rulers with divine attributes is as old as history, and the early seventeenth century still breathed a theological atmosphere. Anglicans and Puritans, democrats and royalists, mixed their theology with their politics, revelled in Biblical precedents and maxims, and demanded divine authority for their theories of government. It thus appeared to many self-evident that as the world was governed by one God, the State should be governed by one man. But the compelling cause and the historical justification of the doctrine of the divine right of kings lay nearer to hand. The arguments used by Dante, Occam, Marsilio, and other defenders of the medieval Emperors against the vaunting claims of the Papacy were adopted by the champions of Protestant kingship against the same powerful foe. The contest with Rome led Luther and his followers to magnify the office and emphasize the sacredness of the representative of national independence. Divine right thus began its career as a defensive weapon against militant Catholicism. An answer was required to the audacious claim of the Pope to depose kings at his will, and to the contention of Catholic publicists that authority resided with the people. Men were eager to find an emotional basis for a strong government in the appeal to a supernatural sanction. To strengthen the Crown was to strengthen the State. It rallied sentiment round the king as the centre and symbol of an organic national life, the guardian of its free and unfettered development. When the Huguenots and Puritans adopted the doctrine of the sovereignty of the people, it appeared to many still more necessary to exalt the person and office of the ruler as a bulwark against foes within and without.

Despite its historical and philosophical sanctions,

B

the doctrine of divine right and its corollary of non-resistance made few converts outside the Anglican clergy before the Civil War, and the ablest Ministers of the first two Stuarts rejected it. It required the blood of Charles, the exclusion of his son and the horrors of anarchy to create that passionate loyalty to the crown which sought natural expression in terms of mystical devotion. Yet though some of the saintliest men of their age were numbered among its champions, it never took deep root in England. In defending the theory against Pope and Puritan they were driven to the support of despotism. In defending the secular power against the ecclesiastical they forgot the danger of the secular ruler himself becoming a tyrant. More-over, its appeal was weakened by the follies of the Stuart kings, and by the growth of political rationalism and theological latitudinarianism throughout Europe. Non-resistance could never satisfy a nation with traditions of constitutional life, rapidly growing in culture and wealth; and after a brief experience of a Catholic king it was abandoned, except by a handful of non-jurors, without a sigh. When a theory forged to resist Catholicism was claimed in its support, it was time to throw it away. With the Revolution of 1688 the theory of an original contract was substituted for that of the divinity of kings, which passed with dramatic suddenness out of English history. 'The doctrine of non-resistance', declares Gardiner in words of unusual severity, 'was false in itself and hung like a blight for many years over the energies of England. If it had ever obtained general recognition, it would have cut at the root of all that has made the nation what it is.'

II

Though the doctrine of the divinity of kings was rarely held outside the ranks of the Anglican Church, the ideal of enlightened absolutism was cherished by some of the strongest intellects of the time. That a great State could be ruled by a Parliament had occurred to no one as possible, and it was the natural doctrine not only of the courtier but of the thinker and of the plain man that the King was the real spokesman and director of the country. Among the champions of a strong and enlightened monarchy by far the greatest was Bacon. His chaplain Rawley, in publishing the *New Atlantis* in 1627, announced that his master had intended to supplement his picture of Solomon's House by a sketch of an ideal commonwealth. 'But foreseeing it would be a long work his desire of collecting the Natural History diverted him, which he preferred by many degrees before it.' It is, however, possible to reconstruct his political ideas from his pamphlets and speeches, his essays and treatises. Though he described himself in the *De Augmentis* as 'a man naturally fitted rather for literature than for anything else, and borne by some destiny against the inclination of his genius into the business of active life', he had as definite a message to deliver in affairs of State as in the realm of thought. But whereas in philosophy he was a pioneer, in politics he was a conservative if not a reactionary.

Bacon's first political utterances appeared in the reign of Elizabeth, and dealt with ecclesiastical questions. The *Advice to Queen Elizabeth*, written about 1585, urged her to modify the oath of allegiance for Catholics while continuing to exclude them from office. At the same time he condemned the acts of the Bishops in the expulsion of Puritan preachers, whose fanaticism, however, he makes no attempt to defend. The ideas of the young lawyer were reiterated and expanded in his *Advertisement touching the Controversies of the Church of England*. Once more he censures both Catholics and Puritans, though his sympathy with the latter, perhaps derived from his mother, is obvious. His desire was for a truly national Church. He values Christianity, but is indifferent to the details of Church government and ceremonial. He pleads for elasticity, and frankly recognizes the need of reform in the Church. We seem to breathe the serene atmosphere of Hooker. A tolerant Erastian, he asks that the State should be supreme and the quarrels of sects be overruled for the welfare of the community. Presbyterianism, he maintained, would be no less prejudicial to the liberties of private men than to the sovereignty of princes. In the great debate on Monopolies in 1601 he declared, 'For the prerogative of the prince, I hope I shall never hear it discussed. The Queen hath both enlarging and restraining power; she may set at liberty things restrained by statute and may restrain things which be at liberty.'

The first ten Essays, issued in 1597, eschew politics; but with the accession of James Bacon made determined efforts to push his way at Court. 'There is no subject', he wrote, 'whose heart is not set on fire to sacrifice itself a burnt-offering to Your Majesty's service, among which no man's fire shall be more pure and fervent than mine.' Despite these fulsome phrases, he sincerely believed that the scholarly ruler would use his power both for the political guidance of his people and for the patronage of science. *The Advancement of Learning*, dedicated to the King in 1605, struck the same note of hopeful adulation. 'I am possessed with an extreme wonder at the largeness of your capacity, the fruitfulness of your memory, the swiftness of your apprehension, the penetration of your judgement and the facility of your elocution. God hath given to your Majesty an understanding able to compass and comprehend the greatest matters and nevertheless to touch and apprehend the least; whereas it should seem an impossibility in nature for the same instrument to make itself fit for great and small works. There hath not been since Christ's time any temporal monarch so learned in all literature and erudition, divine and human.' In the survey of the conquests and aims of learning to which the book is devoted the discussion of politics is very brief, partly because government is in some respects a secret, partly because 'I write to a king that is a master of this science'. Moreover, if he were to live a thousand years, he would never be tempted to disagree with the philosophy of the *True Law of Free Monarchies*. He only reminds his readers that those who have written of laws have written as philosophers or as lawyers, not as statesmen. 'As for philosophers they make imaginary laws for imaginary commonwealths, and their discourses are as the stars, which give little light because they are so high. For the lawyers they write, according to the state where they live, what is received, not what ought to be law; for the wisdom of a lawyer is one, and of a lawmaker another.' Monarchies, he declared in his memorandum in the case of the Post-Nati of Scotland, did not exist by a precedent law or compact. Submission to them was as natural as the obedience of a child to its parents.

Allegiance to hereditary monarchs was the dictate of the law of nature.

Bacon's contempt for lawyers was repeated in many of his political memoranda; and he sided with the King in the skirmishes which filled his reign. While jurists were bound by the past, the monarch could freely consider the needs of the present or future. No amount of legal knowledge, he believed, would make a statesman or fit men to deal with matters of high policy. Prerogative represented the cause of progress in the battle against pedantry and routine. As he conceived it, the monarch was not to break the law, but to rise above it in the interest of the commonwealth. Parliament was also a possible obstacle to progress, for it was an assembly of lawyers. In his *View of the Differences between King's Bench and the Council in the Marches* (1606), he taught that the King could suspend Acts of Parliament and control the common law. His inmost thoughts are revealed with almost brutal frankness in the rough notes jotted down in 1608, known as *Commentarius Solutus*. His contempt for 'mere lawyers' breaks out angrily. He has no objection to Parliaments so long as they do not attempt to control the government; but he suggests that the lawyers, without whom the country gentlemen would be leaderless, should be intimidated by the fear of losing promotion. His policy is to exalt the King's 'summary justice', which will conciliate the poor by cheap and swift law, and to secure a permanent revenue. Though Bacon was a sincere royalist these secret notes leave an unpleasant impression. In exalting the prerogative he frankly desired to further his interests by flattering his master. It is here, too, that the suggestion first occurs to distract attention from internal controversy by foreign aggression. In later years he developed this evil counsel in two pamphlets, one advising a crusade of Catholic and Protestant Powers against the Turk, the other urging a Protestant onslaught on Spain, a State for which he felt an unconquerable distrust. There was a strain of recklessness in Bacon's thought which was restrained neither by moral principles nor by consideration for the enduring interests of his country.

The fullest and most comprehensive statement of his political philosophy is to be found in the Essays added to the editions of 1612 and 1625. The most notable of these utterances, 'Of the true greatness of Kingdoms and Estates', was reproduced in the eighth book of the *De Augmentis*. The ideal is that of a powerful military State, resting on a virile, prosperous and well-armed people. Mercenaries are a broken reed, numbers are of little value without a martial spirit, and taxes must be moderate. 'No people overcharged with tribute is fit for empire. It importeth most that a nation do profess arms as their principal honour, study, and occupation. Moreover, they should ever be ready to spring to arms. Let nations that pretend to greatness sit not too long upon a provocation.' War is necessary for the well-being as for the greatness of kingdoms. 'Nobody can be healthful without exercise, neither natural body nor politic; and certainly to a kingdom or estate a just and honorable war is a true exercise.' A State must be strong on sea as well as on land. 'To be master of the sea is an abridgment of a monarchy.' The train of thought is continued in the essay 'Of Empire'. In foreign relations, declares our philosopher, there is only one general rule. 'Princes must keep due sentinel that none of their neighbours do overgrow so, by increase of territory, by embracing a trade or the like, as they become more able to annoy them than they were.' The true principle of foreign policy is the maintenance of the balance of power. 'The opinion of some of the schoolmen is not to be received that war cannot be made but upon a precedent injury or provocation; for there is no question but a just fear of danger, though there be no blow given, is a lawful cause of a war.' A nationalist of the exclusive school, Bacon was totally lacking in the sense that statesmen and rulers owe allegiance to European civilization and to humanity at large. In this respect he was inferior to his own master and still more to his great contemporary Grotius. The same blindness appears in his well-known economic maxim, 'the increase of any State must be upon the foreigner; for whatever is somewhere gotten is somewhere lost'.

The essay 'Of Seditions' expounds the theory of domestic statecraft. Seditions arise from two groups of causes, from poverty and from discontent. To counteract the former—'for the rebellions of the belly are the worst'—the State must exert its whole strength, intervening in every department of commercial and industrial life, by 'the opening and well-balancing of trade, the cherishing of manufactures, the banishing of idleness, the repressing of waste and excess by sumptuary laws, the improvement and husbanding of the soil, the regulating of prices, the moderating of taxes and tributes'. Above all, wealth must not be gathered into a few hands, lest a State have a great stock and yet starve; for 'money is like muck, not good except it be spread'. A strict hand must therefore be kept on usury, monopoly and great properties. In discussing the second group of causes of sedition he cautions against making the wound bleed inwards; but he has little of a practical character to suggest. A wise government handles things 'so that no evil shall appear so peremptory but that it hath some outlet of hope'. No great personage in the State should be suffered to become a leader of disaffection, and princes should avoid indiscreet sayings which fly abroad like arrows. Finally, rulers should have some great person of military valour near them to suppress seditions before they grow.

None of the Essays speaks of the kingly office with the unction common in the papers intended directly for the King's eye. Indeed, Bacon's real conception was rather of the Tudor than of the Jacobean age, rather of the State as an organism in which King and Parliament possessed their appropriate functions than in which the King was the sole source of power. The State is a cosmos, of which the King is 'the primum mobile which moveth all things'. A monarchy without a nobility is 'a pure and absolute tyranny' like the Turks. But 'it is well when nobles are not too great for sovereignty nor justice, and yet maintained in that height as the insolence of inferiors may be broken upon them, before it come on too fast upon the majesty of kings'. There must be greater and lesser nobles to balance each other. Kings, nobles, merchants, yeomen are the steps in the great hierarchy. In the essay 'Of Judicature' he urges the judges to remember that Solomon's throne was supported by lions on both sides. 'Let them be lions, but lions under the throne, being circumspect they do not check or oppose any points of sovereignty.' Their office is to interpret law, not to make it. It is a happy thing when kings and judges often consult. Let no man imagine antagonism between just laws and true policy.

In the 'Treatise on Universal Justice or the Fountains of Equity', in the eighth book of the *De Augmentis*, he protests against the worship of precedents. The fact that a course was once adopted does not tell so much in its favour as the subsequent abandonment tells against it. 'Examples are to be used for advice, not for rulers and orders.' The King is to be the Moderator in every department of the national life. In the essay 'Of Unity in Religion' he repeats the warnings of his early pamphlets against disputes on trivialities. 'There be two swords among Christians, the spiritual and temporal, and both have their due office and place in the maintenance of religion.' The temporal sword is to be drawn with great circumspection, and must never be put into the hands of the common people. Let that be left to the Anabaptists and other furies. Every weapon, however, must be used to 'damn and send to hell for ever' doctrines encouraging the murder of princes, the butchery of peoples and the subversion of states and governments. What would Lucretius have said had he known of the Bartholomew Massacre and Gunpowder Plot? The Churches must be kept from stirring up discord among people or attacking the State. A generation before Hobbes Bacon taught the unfettered sovereignty of the State alike over the religion and the politics of its citizens.

Bacon's ideal was a State in which the sovereign, though aided by wise counsellors, should be responsible to no one for his actions within the wide and undefined limits of his prerogative. The House of Commons should be frequently summoned to express the complaints and wishes of the country, as well as to assent to new laws and extraordinary taxation. The

King should have a sufficient revenue for ordinary expenses, and should be able to punish those who resisted his authority by some more direct and certain way than trial by jury. Such interferences with the ordinary course of law would, however, be rare. The suggestions of Parliament would be considered by the ruler and the Privy Council, and such as possessed value would be adopted. Parliament possessed neither the knowledge nor the experience to govern the country. Owing confidence to the sovereign, it should not paralyse his arm by attempts to limit his authority or to insist on an explanation of his every act.

The weakness of the system, both as a contribution to the problems of his day and as a guide to the art of statesmanship, was that it depended for its success on the character and capacity of the ruler, and that it overlooked the educative influence of self-government. Though he had abundant opportunity to know the intellectual and moral limitations of his master, he continued to base his edifice on the wisdom of princes. In the chapter on 'The Art of Empire or Civil Government' in the *De Augmentis*, written in 1621, he declares that he has imposed silence on himself, 'though one who has had the benefit of long experience and has been accustomed for eighteen years to the commands and conversations of Your Majesty, whereby a very stock might be turned into a statesman'. It had, however, long become obvious to every one except James himself that he was not fit to rule virtually unaided over a great people. Bacon's fault was that by encouraging such a king to strain the notion of prerogative he pushed him towards a collision which could only end in disaster. But apart from the un-worthiness of James for the role assigned to him, the system itself was unsound. In contemplating the beneficent uses to which the prerogative could be put, he forgot how precarious are the benefits derived from irresponsible power and how degrading such power proves to its holders themselves. In concentrating his vision on an efficient executive he forgot the political education of the people. Moreover, it never occurred to him that the instinct of common men might sometimes be wiser than the wisdom of kings and philosophers. His system, in a word, was suited to a state of society that had already passed away. If in science and speculation his face was turned towards the dawn, as a political thinker his horizon was bounded by the autocratic monarchies of the century of the Reformation. He had no insight into the strength and value of the newer currents that were bearing his countrymen in the direction of a wider and more assured liberty.

CHAPTER II

HOBBES

WHILE James proclaimed the divinity of lawful kings and Bacon preached the ideals of the Tudor monarchy, Hobbes, the author of the first comprehensive political system produced in England, derived his theory of the State neither from theology nor from tradition, but from the study of human nature. The most interesting as well as the most explosive English thinker in the seventeenth century stood aloof from the contending factions. No man of his time occupied such a lonely position in the world of thought, and it was only in the nineteenth century that his importance was fully grasped and the startling modernity of his cardinal principles was realized. While the divine right of kings perished with the theological age which gave it birth, the sovereignty of the State exhibits every characteristic of robust and undiminished vitality.

Born in the year of the Armada, Hobbes learned as little at Oxford as most of his contemporaries. Becoming tutor to the son of the first Earl of Devonshire, with whom he visited France and Italy, he established the happy relations with the Cavendish family which only terminated seventy years later with his death. He enjoyed ample leisure, and roamed at will over the wide expanses of philosophy and classical literature. It was in these years that he made the acquaintance of Bacon, who, as Aubrey records, used to walk up and down the gardens of Gorhambury in contemplation. When an idea entered his mind he would at once communicate it to one of his attendants; and he used to say that Hobbes was quicker than anyone in seizing his meaning and conveying it to paper in an intelligible form. The chief product of his early studies was a translation of Thucydides, whose pregnant analysis of the problems of government commanded his admiration, and whose vivid pictures of political confusion confirmed his conviction of the necessity of a strong ruler. A second and third journey abroad enabled him to study the France of Richelieu at close quarters. In Italy he made the acquaintance of Galileo, and in Paris formed an enduring friendship with Mersenne, the henchman of Descartes, Gassendi and other French scholars. Returning to England in 1638, he associated with the famous group of lawyers, poets, and divines who gathered round Falkland at Great Tew and freely discussed problems of government and religion. He watched the gathering storm, and in 1640 felt impelled to sketch out a political theory differing widely from that held either by King or Parliament.

The little work entitled *The Elements of Law Natural and Politic*, though not written for publication, circulated freely in manuscript copies; and the author later declared that if the Short Parliament had not been dissolved, his life would have been in danger. The Opposition had more serious work on hand than to rend an unknown philosopher; but the timid thinker fled in panic to France, where he remained till Charles had lost his head. The book, which consists of two parts, the first entitled 'Human Nature', the second '*De Corpore Politico*', is distinguished by the clearness and pregnant brevity which he never lost. Though it was directly prompted by the controversies of the day, there is no reference to current events and no trace of polemical purpose. The first part describes the differ-

ent elements in human nature, and urges the necessity
for men to find security against each other. 'The cause
which moveth a man to become subject to another is
the fear of not otherwise preserving himself.' At this
point the second part begins. The state of nature,
which is a state of war, passes into political society
when it is agreed that a majority, or a few or one, shall
represent the will of all, either for a limited time or for
ever. The Government, whatever its nature, must have
the power of coercion; 'for the wills of most men are
governed by fear'. In every State there is an absolute
and indivisible sovereignty, which can neither be
punished nor resisted. Obedience to the sovereign is
terminable only by exile or conquest; for 'every man
may lawfully defend himself that hath no other defence'. Though monarchy is not the only possible form
of government, it is the least subject to passion or to
dissolution by civil war. To avoid uncertainty in the
succession the sovereign may name his successor. He
must also decide controversies in religion, controlling
not, indeed, the consciences of men, but their words
and actions; for he is the immediate ruler of the Church
under Christ, and all other authorities are subordinate
to him. In a chapter on the Causes of Rebellion he
rebukes the contention that in certain cases the sovereign may be resisted. If exceptions are made to the
plain rule of obedience, the door is opened to confusion
and peril. In words which recall the *True Law of Free
Monarchies*, he declares that the ruler is required by
God to rule well and wisely under pain of eternal
death, and that his punishment is the affair of God, not
of man. But while James claimed impunity for lawful
rulers alone, Hobbes claims it for all alike. The distinction of *de jure* and *de facto* is brushed aside. The

duty of the sovereign is to keep men from cutting each others' throats; and that duty can be discharged as efficiently by a usurper as by the anointed descendant of a hundred kings.

It is not surprising that the little treatise impressed its readers; for its doctrines came as a sharp challenge to the parties that were girding themselves for battle in the spring of 1640. The doctrine of indivisible sovereignty and of law as the command of the sovereign had been proclaimed by Bodin during the wars of religion in France; but the idea was still unfamiliar in England. From the votaries of divine right he was separated by his purely secular view of the origin of kingship, and by his refusal to concern himself with the legal title of the sovereign. From the Parliamentary leaders he was still more deeply sundered by his contempt for fundamental laws and by his uncompromising repudiation of limited monarchy. Though both King and Parliament saw some of their cherished convictions assailed, the latter was the more deeply outraged. The message of the book was that the King had the right to do whatsoever he pleased. From the safe anchorage of Paris he followed the crisis with anxious interest, and occupied himself with the composition of the *De Cive*, which appeared in Latin in 1642.

Though the dedication to his patron, the Earl of Devonshire, announces that he is careful not to meddle with the laws of any special nation, the Preface makes it clear that the book was written throughout with English politics in the author's mind. He speaks of the 'errors' that a tyrant may be killed, a prince deposed, a king's commands discussed by private citizens before they obey, and of the fearful mischief they bring in their train. In classical times the supreme power was reverenced and obeyed. 'They little used, as in our days, to join themselves with ambitions and hellish spirits to the utter ruin of the State. They could not entertain so strange a fancy as not to desire the preservation of that by which they were preserved.' The state of nature being a mere war of all against all, instinct compels the desire to escape from 'this misery'. Though monarchy is the most convenient government, the beginning of wisdom is to recognize that in every State there must be a supreme power to which obedience is due in all things, as well spiritual as temporal.

When the *De Cive* was launched Hobbes began a third and still more detailed exposition of his political philosophy. While engaged on the *Leviathan* he was appointed mathematical tutor to the Prince of Wales, and laid the foundation of an acquaintance which was to be of no small value in later years. The execution of the King in 1649 stirred him to offer guidance to his afflicted country. In 1650 he at last allowed the *Elements of Law* to be printed, and in 1651 he published an English translation of the *De Cive*. Later in the same year the *Leviathan* appeared in London. He no longer hid his counsels in Latin, but appealed directly to his fellow countrymen. Shortly after its appearance Charles II reached Paris a hunted fugitive, and was presented by the author with a manuscript copy. Though the gay young King shirked the massive treatise, certain members of the royal circle were more curious and raised such a hue and cry that Hobbes fled from Paris.

In his attack on the *Leviathan*, written many years after in his final exile, Clarendon declared that he had

c

conversed with Hobbes on the eve of the appearance
of the book, and asked him how he could publish such
doctrines. The philosopher replied, half in jest, half
in earnest. 'The truth is I have a mind to go home.'
Even if the conversation is correctly reported it can
only have been a joke; for the principles of the
Leviathan are those of the little treatise of 1640, and
Hobbes was the last man wilfully to risk offending
the King. In like manner the charge brought against
him after the Restoration that the book was 'writ in
defence of Oliver's title' is refuted by dates. While he
was putting the finishing touches to the treatise in
1650, England was governed by the Rump. The real
cause of his expulsion was not his politics, but his
theology and his contemptuous treatment of ecclesiastical pretensions. 'All honest men here', wrote the
King's Secretary, Sir Edward Nicholas, 'are very glad
that the King hath at length banished from his court
that father of atheists Mr. Hobbes.' The philosopher
made his submission to the Council of State, and spent
the remainder of his long life in England.

*The Leviathan or the Matter, Form and Power of a
Commonwealth Ecclesiastical and Civil*, is not only the
fullest presentation of Hobbes's theory of the State,
but one of the great books of the world. Its originality
and power, its clarity of thought and pregnancy of
phrase secure it a place among the classics of political
philosophy beside *The Prince*, the *Essays on Civil
Government* and the *Contrat Social*. The frontispiece
strikes the keynote of the book. A gigantic crowned
figure, with a sword in the right hand and a crozier in
the left, rises behind a hill at the bottom of which lies
a stately city. Above the head of the sovereign are the
resounding words, *Non est potestas super terram quæ*

comparetur ei. The great Leviathan, declares the Introduction, is the State, 'which is but an artificial man, though of greater stature and strength than the natural, for whose protection and defence it was intended'.

The first of the four books deals with Man, and passes in review his faculties and capacities, his virtues and defects. He pronounces men to be by nature so nearly equal in the faculties of mind and body that, while they all long for power, none can claim any benefit to which another may not pretend. From equality proceeds rivalry, and from rivalry proceeds war—not war in the organized sense, but a perpetual struggle of all against all. The desires and passions from which this anarchy arises are in themselves no sin, nor are the actions that result from them a crime till they are forbidden by law. But no laws can be made till men agree who shall make them. The state of primitive society or the state of nature was intolerable—'no industry, no arts, no letters, no society, and continual fear and danger of violent death'. The life of man was 'solitary, poor, nasty, brutish, short'. Notions of right and wrong, justice and injustice, had no place. 'Where there is no common power there is no law; where no law, no injustice.' As the state of nature proved to no one's interest—for the weakest is strong enough to kill the strongest—it was natural that a way of escape should be sought. This could only be attained by every individual surrendering his right to do what he liked to a single man or body of men. Thus the war of all against all was exchanged for political society. The community became a state, the control of which was vested in the sovereign, the Leviathan or mortal God. The contracting parties are not the community and the sovereign, but subject and subject. The sovereign is the result of the pact, not a party to it. Hobbes defends this curious departure from the common theory on the ground that men in a state of nature, acknowledging no common authority, cannot make a contract collectively. The multitude is not a unit, and no 'people' exists till a government has been formed.

The sovereign is chosen and endowed with power in the expectation that he will introduce peace and security; but though his authority is derived exclusively from those over whom he rules, he is bound by no obligations to them. The anti-social instincts of mankind are too insistent to be checked except by absolute authority; and any attack on that authority would involve an instant relapse into the barbarism which was deliberately abandoned. His will is law, and his subjects have only a right to do what he does not forbid. There is no limit to his power, though Hobbes allows an individual to resist an attempt to kill, wound or imprison him. The covenant once made cannot be terminated or revised. As he embodies the will of all, his actions are virtually their actions. A limited monarchy is a contradiction in terms. His task is to protect his subjects against foreign enemies and internal commotions, to decide on war and peace, and to levy the necessary taxation. The law embodies his command, and he must decide on its interpretation. He must suppress the publication of opinions which he deems dangerous to social peace. As he was instituted to defend the people against themselves, he must perform his task in his own way and without let or hindrance.

In the *Leviathan*, as in its predecessors, Hobbes

takes infinite pains to establish that the sovereign is supreme, not less in spiritual than in temporal affairs. He will suffer no rival near the throne. Such subordination was, of course, implicit in his theory of the original contract; but his conviction of its necessity was emphasized by the claims of his Catholic and Puritan contemporaries. His gospel was the indivisibility of sovereignty, and sacerdotal pretensions to a co-ordinate or even subordinate authority were sternly repudiated. He trains his heaviest artillery against the claims of the Roman Church, because he realizes the strength of its insidious appeal. The spiritual authority finds its opportunity in the weakness of the average man, with whom 'the fear of darkness and ghosts is greater than other fears', and whose nerves are agitated by the threat of everlasting damnation. Against such a danger the sovereign must defend himself and his subjects, lest there be a struggle in every man's breast between the Christian and the subject. Naked Erastianism forms a vital part of the system; but Hobbes goes further than his argument actually requires. He endeavours to show that there never was a divinely instituted spiritual authority independent of the State, and that even among the Jews the secular sovereign was supreme. The Christian Church only obtained legal status by the gift of the Emperor, and its claim to supernatural authority is therefore baseless. Priests increased their power by encouraging the tendency to superstition latent in every man. He adds the celebrated sentence that has been quoted by a hundred Protestant historians: 'If a man consider the original of this great ecclesiastical dominion, he will easily perceive that the Papacy is no other than the ghost of the deceased Roman Empire sitting crowned upon the grave thereof.' Behind the elaborate parade of Scriptural texts it is easy to detect not only an indignant repudiation of ecclesiastical pretensions, but something like contempt for the dogmas of the Churches. He would have welcomed Gibbon's historic sneer that all religions were to the believer equally true, to the philosopher equally false, to the magistrate equally useful. Religion was of value when it was employed, not to challenge the decisions of the State, but to teach men to live in peace.

If the rule of 'Leviathan' should seem as intolerable as the anarchy from which it offered an escape, the reply was that the Government would interfere but little in the routine of daily life. While possessing the right and power to determine every detail, it would in practice permit whatever did not tend to disturb the peace. The laws should be few and simple. 'As nature ordained the banks not to stay but to guide the course of a stream, so it is against sound policy that there should be more laws than necessarily serve for the good of the magistrate and his subjects.' In like manner, while the expression of opinion was subject to the will of the sovereign, thought itself remained free. There must be outward conformity to the worship ordained by law; but a man might believe as much or as little as he liked. For instance, he might reject 'those acts that have been given out for miracles'. There was, in fact, no need to molest a conforming sceptic like the philosopher of Malmesbury.

The *Leviathan* provoked an outburst of indignation in royalist and ecclesiastical circles, and hard words were used of its audacious author. They detested his anticlericalism, his secularism, his contempt for the Universities. They were incensed by his doctrine that

theology was a branch of politics, not politics of
theology. For many years every sort of scepticism or
free-thought was denounced as Hobbism. Evelyn
records that the gentle physicist, Robert Boyle, entertained feelings of antipathy for but one person in the
world, and that was Hobbes. Bentley was later to
ascribe the decay of morality to Hobbes, and Dr.
Sacheverell to class him with Spinoza as an atheistical
monster. Hobbes's dislike of the clergy was only
equalled by their detestation of him. The most substantial and authoritative reply came from the greatest
of royalists. The *Brief View of the Dangerous and
Pernicious Errors to Church and State in Mr. Hobbes's
book*, written by Clarendon in exile in 1670, was
dedicated to Charles II. 'I could not think of anything
of more importance to Your Majesty's service than to
confute Hobbes.' To his personal worth he offers a
warm testimonial. 'A man of excellent parts, of great
wit, of some reading and somewhat more thinking,
Hobbes is one of the most ancient acquaintances I
have in the world, and of whom I have always had a
great esteem as one who, besides his eminent parts of
learning and knowledge, hath been always looked upon
as a man of probity and a life free from scandal.' To
his teaching, however, he shows no mercy. Liberty,
religion and justice were only empty words. Moreover, his theory of the contract did not even close the
door to rebellion. If there was a revolt the ruler could
not complain, for his subjects thereby broke no promise
made to him. The old exile naturally repudiates the
doctrine that a usurper once possessed of the sceptre
should be implicitly obeyed. If a subject might and must
submit to his new master as soon as the old one was
unable to protect him, loyalty was torn up by its roots.

The contemptuous treatment of religion provokes scarcely less indignation. He concludes with a wish that it should be burnt. 'I never read any book which contained so much sedition, treason and impiety.'

Passing from contemporary controversialists, a modern critic would begin by challenging the foundation on which the system rests. The necessity for absolute government is stated over and over again to lie in human nature itself as revealed in primitive society. But neither Hobbes nor his contemporaries knew anything of the actual life of primitive communities. His terrifying picture of a war of all against all corresponds to no reality. No community lives or could live in the state which he describes. For Hobbes there is no middle term between anarchy and absolutism. He was not aware that custom preceded law, and that the sanction of the one is as potent as of the other. He rightly rejected sentimental rhapsodies on the noble savage and the golden age of innocence and virtue; but he was unaware that the elements of social life are never absent among human beings, and that savages possess a rudimentary morality without any political organization. The unit of primitive society was not, as he imagined, the individual, but the family or some other group, and the life of primitive man was far more fettered by tradition and rule than that of England under the Stuart kings. Progress towards a more complex organization occurred not because the conditions were unbearable, but owing to the emergence of new needs and aptitudes, often stimulated by peaceful or hostile intercourse with other communities. Hobbes expressly declares that in drawing a darkly shadowed picture of early society he is bringing no indictment against human nature; but in focusing

attention on self-preservation he completely overlooks
the complementary instinct of mutual aid. For him
man is neither a moral nor a political animal. Behind
every theory of absolute government lurks a disparag-
ing view of mankind, and Hobbes is no exception to
the rule.

With the destruction of his vision of primitive
society the case for the iron yoke of a Leviathan falls
to the ground. But even assuming the necessity of
escaping from an unbearable situation, Hobbes fails
to convince his readers that the only course was the
unconditional surrender of 'natural' rights. In his
famous treatise *De Rege*, the Spanish Jesuit Mariana,
who anticipated Hobbes in his description of the state
of nature and traced civil society to the failings of
mankind, declared that the community reserved more
power than it surrendered. Hooker, again, who had
shared the view that the compact was between the
members of the group, not between ruler and subject,
had declined to draw the inference that they had
beggared themselves. His argument that no collective
action was possible is controverted by his own version
of events. The determination to escape from the state
of nature was a collective volition, and the transference
of rights to a sovereign was a collective action. His
contention that men parted with their natural rights
without the smallest security for the future is an affront
to common sense. If men were capable of contracting
out of their rights towards one another, they were
equally capable of giving general directions to the
ruler of their choice. The doctrine of the original
contract in its usual form, though a pure fiction, found
favour for many centuries precisely because it satisfied
the sense of equity. It proclaimed the gospel of govern-

ment by consent. As subjects owed a reasonable obedience to the ruler, so the ruler owed good government to his subjects. No unconditional and irrecoverable surrender of natural rights could take place. Some were surrendered in order to guarantee the rest. No generation could bind its successors for ever. The same demand for a better life which led to the selection of a ruler carried with it the right to test his actions by the measure in which they secured that object. In Hobbes's scheme, on the other hand, neither subject nor sovereign undertakes any obligations to the other.

The theory of an absolute sovereign, as has been pointed out, was almost equally unacceptable to the contending factions into which England was divided while Hobbes was writing his treatises. Clarendon speaks bitterly of his 'notorious ignorance in the law and constitution of England'; and indeed the spirit is rather that of a Continental than a British publicist. He was wrong in his contention that there is and always must be a sovereign in every State. There was no sovereignty in his sense in the Middle Ages, when power was divided between Church and State, between the King and his feudatories. His conviction that mixed government involves anarchy has been disproved by experience. Yet his doctrine, which seemed so extravagant in the seventeenth century, was capable of adaptation in the circumstances of a widely different age. Though he repeatedly spoke of monarchy as the 'most commodious' form of government, he declares that the sovereign might be a king or an assembly. His mission was to attack the division of power. With whom that power rested was of minor importance. Thus a doctrine which sounded almost monstrous when predicated of a single man would wear a very different aspect when applied to a representative assembly; and the fame of Hobbes, after a long period of obscuration, was revived by the Philosophic Radicals of the early nineteenth century. The division of power between king and Parliament was, as he maintained, a source of danger; and the only means of terminating it was to settle which should be supreme. The events of 1688 having finally decided against the King, Parliament gradually came to occupy the position of undisputed sovereign. The conditions of Hobbes are fulfilled not less by a democratic Parliament in a country which possesses no written constitution than by the monarchy of Louis XIV. This capacity for adaptation to totally different circumstances distinguishes his position from that of his royalist contemporaries.

A further aspect of his teaching is also strangely modern. Hobbes recognized no law but the will of the actual sovereign. 'Laws of nature' were simply 'rules of reason', generalisations from experience, principles discovered to be essential to life and prosperity, but possessing in themselves no power of securing recognition. While paying lip-service to the authority of Scripture, he reserved to the sovereign the monopoly of its interpretation. He rejects, moreover, the appeal both to fundamental laws of a peculiarly sacred character, such as Magna Charta, and to precedent. Like Halifax, Burke, and Bentham, he teaches that the powers of government must be based on the needs of society, not on any theory of primitive rights. In the *Dialogue of the Common Laws*, written in old age, he remarks concisely that it is not wisdom but authority that makes a law. Laws made in past times have no validity without the approval and

support of the reigning sovereign. Of the Law of
Nature, on which thinkers of many schools erected
their structure and by which they tested existing
conditions, Hobbes will hear nothing; for, assuming
it to exist, it could be interpreted by every man in his
own way, and a conflict would at once arise between
natural and positive law. The doctrine that law is
the command of a superior, and that no law can be
recognized which is not enforceable by punishment,
was taken over bodily by Austin and forms the kernel
of his teaching.

The worst part of Hobbes's system is that it allows
the State no positive function. Its sole duty is the
maintenance of order. 'Leviathan' is the policeman,
not the instructor. He has no vision of the Greek ideal
of a State as a work of art, or of Burke's splendid conception of an association in all science, in all art, in all
perfection. He accepts the Aristotelian maxim that
the State comes into being that man may live, but
ignores the equally vital truth that it continues in order
that he may live well. His State is a necessary evil, an
instrument to defend men against their savage instincts,
not to achieve a free and progressive civilisation. His
ideal was the rigid absolutism of the Bourbons, not
freedom slowly broadening down from precedent to
precedent.

When Hobbes returned to England in 1651 and
made his peace with the Commonwealth, he was acting
in strict consistency with his teaching. Directly a
sovereign ceased to be able to protect his subjects, his
claim to their allegiance was at an end. Though the
Leviathan was not written in the interest of the
Commonwealth, its counsels of submission to a *de
facto* government were highly opportune. In 1656

the philosopher claimed credit for 'turning the minds of a thousand gentlemen to a conscientious obedience to the present government, which otherwise would have wavered'. Though he detested the confusion which followed the Protector's death, the approach of the Restoration aroused lively apprehensions for his safety. But though he had many enemies at Court he possessed a steady friend in Charles II, who recognized his old tutor in the streets on his arrival in London and raised his hat in kindly greeting. Loving the society of wits, he ordered that the veteran thinker should be admitted whenever he appeared at Court, and used to greet him with the words, 'Here comes the bear to be baited'. 'After the King's return', records Clarendon, 'he came frequently to the Court, where he had too many disciples, and he once visited me.' Though the omnipotent minister hated both his absolutism and his scepticism, men of less austerity delighted in the company of one who, in the words of his devoted friend Aubrey, was 'marvellous happy and ready in his replies'. With the rising tide of reaction, however, his position became increasingly insecure; and when the Plague and the Great Fire upset the nerves of the public, a Bill was introduced to suppress atheism and profaneness, and a committee was chosen to examine the *Leviathan*. Though the Bill, which passed the Commons, was dropped, Hobbes, always timid and now an old man of seventy-eight, was thoroughly scared. He burned some of his papers, wrote an essay to prove that he could not be lawfully executed for heresy, and ostentatiously attended the private chapel of the Earl of Devonshire. The King prevented his enemies proceeding to extremities, but forbade him to publish any more controversial books.

Hobbes's last important work, *Behemoth, or a Dialogue on the Civil Wars*, written in 1668, was printed without his knowledge a few months before his death in 1679, from an imperfect copy of his manuscript. The work is extraordinarily fresh and vigorous for a man of eighty, and it is of considerable interest for his judgement of the earth-shaking events of the middle decades of the century. While naturally attributing the main responsibility for the catastrophe to the champions of Parliament, he sharply castigates the royalists who thought the government of England was not an absolute but a mixed monarchy and attempted to impose limitations on the prerogative. The attack on the constitutional lawyers was repeated in the *Dialogue of the Common Laws*, written about the same time. Once again he states that the King is the supreme judge and the sole legislator, and that he cannot be controlled by his subjects. Yet it was by a sound instinct that the champions of authority looked askance at the prophet of absolutism; for Hobbes was above all a rationalist, and rationalism is the mortal foe of the mysticism on which the bolder claims of kings and Churches ultimately rest. To a far greater degree than Bacon he was the author of the atmospheric change which substituted the secular for the theological standpoint throughout the boundless realms of thought and speculation.

CHAPTER III

LAW *VERSUS* PREROGATIVE

THE system of government by prerogative preached and practised by James, Charles and Bacon was shattered by the combined resistance of the lawyers and the Puritans. The opposition to James was mainly the work of the former, that to his son mainly of the latter.

I

Edward Coke, the leader of the lawyers' opposition, had served successively under Elizabeth as Speaker and Attorney-General, and had distinguished himself both for ability and rancour in the State trials of Essex, the Gunpowder conspirators, and Raleigh. His temper was as harsh as his language; but though he had few friends his mastery of law, which was universally recognized, made him one of the leading personages of the realm. Between 1600 and 1615 he published eleven volumes of Reports of cases which he had heard. As the main points were brought into bold relief and accompanied by a commentary, each Report was virtually a concise treatise on some department of law, and the volumes quickly won the place in legal studies which they have never lost.

On his appointment to be Chief Justice of the Common Pleas in 1606, the second and greater chapter in Coke's life begins. He had hitherto appeared mainly as a defender of the Crown against the dangers of conspiracy. He was now to emerge as the resolute champion of the Courts of Common Law against the

encroachments of the King. The first conflict arose
in 1607 in reference to the attempt of Bancroft and the
Church, backed by the King, to obtain judicial independence for the ecclesiastical courts. The Archbishop appealed to James on the plea that the judges
were merely the King's delegates, and that he could
remove causes from their jurisdiction and determine
them himself. This doctrine was flatly contradicted
by Coke, who gleefully records the passage at arms in
his Twelfth Report. The King remarked that the law
was founded on reason, and that he possessed reason
as well as the judges. Coke answered that, though the
King was richly endowed by nature, he was not
learned in the laws of England. Causes concerning the
life and fortunes of his subjects, he continued, were
not to be decided by natural reason, but by a knowledge
of law, which required prolonged study and experience.
The law was the golden metewand which tried the
causes of his subjects, and protected the King in safety
and peace. 'With which he was greatly offended, and
said he should then be under the law, which was
treason to affirm. To which I said, "Bracton saith,
'*Quod rex non debet esse sub homine sed sub Deo et
lege.*' " '

Three years later the authority of the law was more
publicly vindicated. A dictionary of legal terms,
entitled *The Interpreter*, had been published by Cowell,
Reader in Civil Law at Cambridge, under the patronage
of Bancroft. 'He is above the law by his absolute
power', wrote Cowell under the heading 'King'; 'and
though for the better course in making laws he do
admit the three estates, yet this is not of constraint,
but of his own benignity. And though at his coronation he take an oath not to alter the laws of the land,

yet, this oath notwithstanding, he may alter or suspend any particular law that seemeth hurtful to the public estate.' Under 'Prerogative' we read, 'By the custom of this Kingdom he maketh no laws without the consent of the three estates, though he may quash any law concluded by them. I hold that the King of England is an absolute King.' Acting, it was believed, on the instigation of Coke, the Commons invited the Lords to join in directing the King's attention to the book. At this moment, however, it was announced that the King was himself displeased with Cowell on the ground that in opposing the prerogative to the law he attacked both King and Parliament. The book was suppressed, but James refused to allow the writer to be punished. But though the sovereign had repudiated the unconsidered phraseology of a supporter, he had no intention of allowing his wings to be clipped. Much could be done by proclamations, the exact authority of which was in doubt. In the same year, 1610, Coke was asked whether the King could by proclamation prohibit the erection of new buildings in or near London and forbid the manufacture of starch from wheat. He insisted on consulting his colleagues, whose united judgement was that the King could not create an offence by proclamation and could only exhort his subjects to observe the law. They added that he possessed no other prerogative than the law allowed him. James kept the opinion of the judges secret, and for a time proclamations imposing punishments ceased to appear. Though the practice was revived, its illegality was definitely established by the judgement of Coke and his three colleagues.

James now recognized the great lawyer as the most formidable opponent of his claims; and in 1613 he

D

adopted Bacon's advice to transfer him to the Chief
Justiceship of the King's Bench, which involved a loss
of income and of influence. But even in this position
his rugged personality made itself felt, and in 1616 he
was dismissed from the Bench. It was with Coke in
his mind that the King at this moment addressed the
Judges in the Star Chamber. 'Encroach not upon the
prerogative of the Crown. If there falls out a question
that concerns my prerogative or mystery of State, deal
not with it till you consult with the King or his council
or both; for they are transcendent matters. As for the
absolute prerogative of the Crown, that is no subject
for the tongue of a lawyer, nor is lawful to be disputed.'
There was now war to the knife. In 1620 Coke re-
entered Parliament, became the real leader of the
Opposition, and was sent to the Tower for nine months
for his share in the protest which the King tore out of
the Commons' Journals in 1621. He lived to inspire the
Petition of Right, and died in 1634 at the age of eighty-
two. His later years were occupied with the production
of his *Institutes*, the first of which was published in
1628, the second, third, and fourth after his death.

In ordinary times Coke would have been a defender
of authority, for he was one of the most conservative
men who ever lived. More than any royalist of his
time he believed in the wisdom of our ancestors. He
deemed it the duty of Parliament to declare and defend
the law, not to make it; and when new principles had
to be applied, he pretended that they were part of a
pre-existing code. It was the supreme duty of Crown
and Parliament to follow precedent. The law of
England was a religion, and he was its high priest, the
interpreter of its mysteries and the defender of its
sanctity. Yet this man, with his repellent personality

and his narrow view of liberty, was one of the founders of constitutional government. It was too early to confront the King with the claim of Parliament to control the executive, and the only effective obstacle to a virtually unlimited prerogative was the majesty of the law. The doctrine which Fortescue had proclaimed under the Lancastrian monarchy was repeated by his admiring successor under the Stuarts. Though there was an element of personal vanity in his ambition to be Grand Arbitrator between the King and the people, his boundless knowledge, his unflinching courage and his passionate earnestness made him the most formidable opponent of autocracy. If he did not aid his countrymen to conquer new liberties, he did more than any other man to secure that they should preserve unimpaired such as they already possessed.

Coke's system was useful in a transitional period, but it possessed none of the elements of finality. In the early seventeenth century there were three claimants to sovereignty—the King, the King in Parliament, and the Law. Only a few extreme men attributed sovereignty to the King alone, the judges in the Ship Money case only declaring that he could dispense with a law 'in cases of necessity'. On the other hand, it was impossible for anyone at that time to hold Parliament to be sovereign, since it came at his call and went at his bidding. The best claimant to sovereignty was the King in Parliament; but this also outraged Coke's sense of the sacredness of tradition. Coke himself thought of Parliament mainly as a court. In his Fourth Institute, on the Jurisdiction of Courts, the first chapter is devoted to the High Court of Parliament. The famous passage in which he speaks of its power and jurisdiction for making laws as 'so transcendent and absolute as it cannot be confined, either for causes or persons, within any bounds', has often been taken to claim political and legislative sovereignty for Parliament; but the instances of its power which he gives refer to the domain of private law. While the Parliamentary party was often to use precedents relating to judicial supremacy to buttress the claim to legislative sovereignty, Coke always limited Parliamentary power by common law. For him the common law was the true sovereign, supreme alike over King and Parliament, prerogative and statute. 'Magna Charta', he declared in the Second Institute, devoted to the Statutes, 'is such a fellow that he will have no sovereign.' Judges might, however, hold even a statute void on the ground that it was contrary to reason or to natural law or to prerogative. If his claim had been granted, lawyers would have become lawgivers. It was too paradoxical to become a constitutional theory, and its acceptance would have substituted one yoke for another. The rule of the law meant the rule of the lawyers. Coke happened to interpret the law in a popular sense; but another might mould it to the purposes of autocracy. The idea of the sovereignty of the law as an esoteric science interpreted by professional jurists died with its great author, and the real struggle began between King and Parliament. The problem was one of power, not of precedent, and it was destined to be solved, not by antiquarian learning, but by the sword.

II

While Coke represented, above all, the Inns of Court, the first great champion of Parliament was a country gentleman of wide culture and ample means. Though called to the Bar, Sir John Eliot did not practise. Entering the House as a young man, it was to him more than to any other member that Charles's determination to rule without Parliaments was due. He led the attack on Buckingham with extraordinary power, and in his celebrated speech on the impeachment compared him to Sejanus. 'Then I must be Tiberius', remarked the King, and sent him to the Tower. The attack on the Duke was not only a blow struck at a hated minister, but an implicit demand that the King's advisers should possess the confidence of Parliament. Quickly released, he returned to the fighting line and took the foremost part in the fierce struggles of 1628–9. 'None', he declared in prophetic terms, 'none have gone about to break Parliaments, but in the end Parliaments have broken them.' He was again sent to the Tower, and this time no appeal from the prisoner or his friends availed to open its portals. His health gave way, and he died in 1632 at the age of forty-two, as much a victim to the King's animosity as if he had perished on the scaffold.

Eliot, like Raleigh, employed his enforced leisure in study and composition. His chief works were two constitutional treatises, into which he poured his learning, his experience and his reflections. They reveal wide knowledge of history and literature, and indicate clearly his own political position. The first, *De Jure Magistratis*, written during the early days of his captivity, displays an astonishingly conservative attitude towards the rights of monarchy. He entertains an almost superstitious reverence for kings. He decisively rejects the contention that subjects may rebel if the sovereign breaks the contract, for they could always discover or invent a pretext, and anarchy would ensue. Moreover, he affirms that the coronation oath is not a contract, since the King is the father of his people, and fathers do not make contracts with their children. The Commonwealth, he declares, is the King's pupil. Varying the metaphor, he compares him to a physician, who may burn or cut a member for the safety of the whole body. 'In case of necessity the King may impose hard things upon his subjects, though it be against the positive and written laws.' On the other hand, he remarks that a king is only the administrator, not the owner of the country, and, with an obvious glance at his relentless enemy in Whitehall, declares that mortal men, when they exalt themselves most proudly, are nearest their downfall.

His second work, *The Monarchy of Man*, was written during the closing months of his life and represents a notable advance. He repeats his emphatic preference for monarchy even over an ideal republic, and admits the existence of prerogative. He adds, however, that it is 'a point so tender that it will hardly bear mention, lest it reflect some new terror on ourselves'. His references to the law, which is hailed as the guardian of freedom, suggest the influence of Coke. The subject, he declares, is free from all but the law, which is 'the king and governor of all things'. He speaks with biting contempt of the flatterers of kingly power. 'There is such labour to make a monarchy unlimited, such distortion of authorities, that to attempt against it is to row against the tide.' He summons a troop of witnesses to prove that the law is above the prince, and contends that rulers find their honour in its supremacy. 'Submission to the law is greater than authority, for it is the ground of all authority.' Princes embody the law, and in being subject to it they are in reality subject to themselves. It is obvious from these treatises that the author was broadly content with the Tudor theory of monarchy. He had no desire to limit the prerogative too closely, and conceded the reserve power of meeting great emergencies, such as invasion or rebellion, claimed by the Stuart kings. He asks for the right of Parliament to counsel, not to execute nor to control. He believed the evil to lie in the person of the monarch, not in the system itself. With a wise and tactful king, who admitted no Somersets or Buckinghams to his closet and ruled in harmony with Parliament, all would be well. His writings supply unimpeachable evidence that in the English no less than in the French Revolution the Opposition was only converted to radical principles by the errors and misdeeds of the government.

III

A more interesting personality than Coke or Eliot, though a less influential politician, was Selden. While Coke confined himself to the law of England, his spacious mind ranged over all nations, ancient and modern. Winning high reputation as a jurist in early manhood, he was often invited to advise Parliament on questions of prerogative, and his share in framing the protest of 1621 was rewarded by a short term of imprisonment. Entering Parliament in 1624, at the age of forty, he joined in the attack on Buckingham and helped to draw up the Petition of Right. He was committed to the Tower in 1629 with Eliot and other leaders, and not released till 1631. His high character and his reputation as the most learned Englishman of his time made him a formidable warrior in the ranks of the Parliamentary Opposition.

The passion of Selden's life was opposition to clerical pretensions. In 1618 he published a *History of Tithes*, in which both his learning and his convictions found expression. Adopting a transparent mask of humility, he declared that the question whether tithes existed by divine right was above his comprehension, and that such problems should be left to canonists. None the less, his own opinion emerged clearly enough in his facts and conclusions. He could discover no evidence that they had been claimed as of right during the first four Christian centuries, and in subsequent ages the practice had been subject to local customs and laws. The upshot of the inquiry was that they had been paid subject to such limitations as the State had imposed. Under the guise of a piece of historical research, he had struck a resounding blow at ecclesiastical claims. The clergy rose in arms, and scented danger both to the security of their incomes and to the existence of the Church. They besought the King to intervene; but James, whose own prerogative was not at issue, showed no desire to punish a man whose learning he respected. After long delay, he allowed the High Commission to order Selden to express regret for having supplied arguments against the divine right of tithes. The great scholar, who had no taste for martyrdom, had no alternative but to submit, and the sale of the book was prohibited. Moreover, when clerical antagonists issued refutations, he was forbidden to reply.

In the year of publication of the *History of Tithes* Selden, at the wish of the King, wrote his *Mare Clausum*, in reply to Grotius' *Mare Liberum*. The contention that the sea was private property, like land, was preposterous; but it delighted James, and when re-written and published in 1636 it delighted his son. Of far higher value were his books on Syrian Religion and on the Greek Inscriptions of the Arundel marbles. His learning and wit made him a favourite in many circles, and he spent pleasant hours as the guest of Laud at Lambeth. Clarendon's Autobiography records the ineffaceable impression he made on men whose paths were to diverge widely from his own. 'Mr. Selden was a person whom no character can flatter or transmit in any expressions equal to his merit and virtue. He was of so stupendous learning in all kinds and in all languages that a man would have thought he had been entirely conversant amongst books and had never spent an hour but in reading and writing. Yet his humanity, courtesy and affability was such that he would have been thought to have been bred in the best Courts, but that his good nature, charity and delight in doing good and communicating all he knew exceeded that breeding. Mr. Hyde was wont to say that he valued himself upon nothing more than upon having had Mr. Selden's acquaintance from the time he was very young.'

Elected for Oxford University to the Long Parliament, Selden supported the great series of measures that brought the system of Personal Government toppling down; but he opposed the impeachment of Strafford and supported Parliament without enthusiasm. Early in 1642 the King thought of offering him the Great Seal, but was told by Hyde and Falkland that it was useless. 'They did not doubt of Mr. Selden's affection to the King', writes Clarendon, 'but withal they knew him so well that they concluded he would absolutely refuse the place. He had for many years enjoyed his ease, which he loved; was rich, and would not have made a journey to York or have lain out of his own bed for any preferment.' There were deeper reasons, not mentioned by Clarendon, which would have prevented the acceptance of the offer. He had no sort of doubt that the conduct of the King had released his subjects from their obedience and that the quarrel had gone so far that it must be settled by arms. ' 'Tis hard to make an accommodation between the King and the Parliament', he remarked. 'If I said I owed you twenty pounds in silver and you said I I owed you twenty pounds in diamonds, 'tis impossible we should ever agree.' But the war itself seemed to him a 'scuffle' in which he could not wholeheartedly support either side. One of the reasons for his luke-warm support of the Parliamentary cause was the growth of a tyrannical Presbyterianism. As a member of the Westminster Assembly, of which Presbyterians formed the majority, he found a fine field for his learning and his wit. Though a Churchman, he had no love for the clergy, and his feelings towards Non-conformist ministers were even less friendly. 'He was like a thorn in their sides', records Anthony Wood, 'for he was able to run them all down with his Greek and antiquities.' Whitelocke describes how he would say, 'It may be so in your little pocket Bibles, but the original is otherwise'. Baillie, the most active of the Scottish delegates, bitterly complains of his antagon-ism. 'Selden and others will have no discipline at all in any Church *jure divino*, but settled only upon the free will and pleasure of Parliament.' In the Westminster Assembly, as in the *History of Tithes*, he was the immovable and scornful Erastian.

Selden's voluminous works, written in Latin and floundering in their own erudition, are forgotten. Even Clarendon admits that his style was harsh and sometimes obscure. 'But in his conversation he was the most clear discourser and had the best faculty of making hard things easy of any man that hath been known.' Fragments of his racy and delightful conversation have been preserved in his *Table-Talk*, which Johnson declared the best book of its kind and Coleridge pronounced to contain more weighty bullion sense than the same number of pages of any uninspired writer. As a treasury of worldly wisdom it ranks with Bacon's Essays. The notes were made by his secretary Milward between 1634 and his death in 1654, and prepared for the press shortly after, though not published till the Revolution of 1688 made their appearance safe. There is no means of dating the utterances, nor do we know if other records were made and destroyed. It is, moreover, highly improbable that these *obiter dicta* were revised by Selden himself. There are singularly few references to current events, and none either to the execution of the King or the reign of Cromwell. 'Wise men', he remarked, 'say nothing in dangerous times.' Yet the greater part of the *Table-Talk* is devoted to religion and politics, and it is not difficult to reconstruct his philosophy.

Selden was a thorough rationalist in politics, and his treatment of the royal office is eminently matter-of-fact. 'Never king dropped out of the clouds', he remarks in his terse manner. 'A king is a thing men have made for their own selves, for quietness' sake, just as in a family one man is appointed to buy the meat.' 'There is no species of kings. A king that claims privileges in his own country because they have them in another is just as a cook that claims fees in one lord's house because they are allowed in another. If the master of the house will yield them, well and good.' Monarchy was simply a constitutional form, and the monarch was as much bound by contract as his subjects. 'To know what obedience is due to the prince you must look into the contract betwixt him and his people; as if you would know what rent is due from the tenant to the landlord, you must look into the lease. When the contract is broken and there is no third person to judge, then the decision is by arms.' But extreme popular claims also excited his scorn. 'The Parliament men are as great princes as any in the world, when whatsoever they please is privilege of Parliament. No man must know the number of their privileges, and whatsoever they dislike is breach of privilege.'

Selden's sharpest arrows are directed against the clergy. 'The priests of Rome', he declares, 'aim but at two things, to get power from the king and money from the subject.' 'Before a juggler's tricks are discovered, we admire him and give him money; but afterwards we care not for them. So 'twas before the discovery of the juggling of the Church of Rome.' Passing to Protestantism, he pronounces Presbyters to have the greatest power of any clergy in the world, and to gull the laity most. He accepts episcopacy as a convenient form of government while scouting its claim to divine institution; 'for in the beginning bishops and presbyters were alike'. Again, he prefers the Prayer Book to 'praying by the spirit'. ' 'Tis hoped we may be cured of our extempore prayers, the same way the grocer's boy is cured of eating plums, when we have had our bellyful of them.' 'Chain up the clergy on both sides', he cries. He compares Convocation to a court-leet, where they have power to make by-laws, 'as that a man shall put so many cows or sheep in the common; but they can make nothing that is contrary to the laws of the kingdom'. 'There's no such thing as spiritual jurisdiction; all is civil.' 'A priest has no such thing as an indelible character. He is made a priest by designation as a lawyer is called to the bar.' ' 'Tis a vain thing to talk of an heretic; for a man can think no otherwise than he does. In primitive times there were many opinions. One of these being embraced by some prince the rest were condemned as heresies; and his religion is said to be orthodox.' 'Religion is like the fashion. One man wears his doublet slashed, another laced, another plain, but every man has a doublet. We differ about the trimming.' 'They say the Holy Ghost is president of their General Councils, when the truth is the odd man is the Holy Ghost.' 'Is the Church or the scripture', he asks, 'judge of religion? In truth neither, but the State. Pretending religion and the law of God is to set all things loose.' Though Sir Matthew Hale testifies that Selden was a resolved, serious Christian, such passages reveal that the heights and depths of religious experience were beyond his vision.

Selden's outlook on life was extraordinarily modern. He was a consistent utilitarian, judging everything by results, and scoffing at all appeals to supernatural sanctions for claims to power, property, or privilege. In ecclesiastical affairs he was a pure Hobbist, and the two men, who keenly relished one another's company, did much to secularize the thought of their time. In politics he was by temperament and conviction a Trimmer, disliking despotism in all its different shapes, and believing in a constitutional monarchy. Though a student rather than a man of action, the ceaseless play of his cool and sceptical intelligence helped to undermine veneration for Church and King, and encouraged men to judge established institutions and ideas in the dry light of reason and common sense. The first Whig was not Shaftesbury, but Selden.

CHAPTER IV

PARLIAMENT, THE ARMY, AND THE PEOPLE

I

CHARLES and his advisers knew little of the real state of public opinion when they were compelled to summon Parliament in 1640. 'The people', Strafford had recently written, 'are in great quietness, and, if I be not much mistaken, well satisfied if not delighted with his Majesty's gracious government and protection.' 'Every man', relates Sir Philip Warwick, 'sat quiet under his own vine, and the fountain of justice ran clear and current.' 'We know not what a rebel is, nor treason', declared Sir Henry Wotton in 1638; 'the names themselves are antiquated with the things.' Believing this to be the case, royalists naturally attributed the events that followed to the incorrigible wickedness of man. 'It arose', said Bishop Hall in a sermon before the King, 'from men who took pleasure in the embroiling of States.' 'Peace, wealth and a model king', wrote Clarendon, 'could but enable, not compel us to be happy. Every man was more troubled at what they called the violation of one law than delighted with the observation of all the rest of the Charter. Nothing less than a universal apostasy in the whole nation from their religion and allegiance could in so short a time have produced such a total and prodigious alteration and confusion over the whole kingdom.'

In so far as this reading of history denied the existence of deep-rooted causes of the great revolt it was childish; but in its testimony to the outward suddenness of the crisis it is approximately correct.

Not a voice was raised against the more important
privileges of the Monarchy, much less against the
Monarchy itself. Neither the Short nor the Long
Parliament at their assembling in 1640 contained a
single Republican. Their task was to strike down
Strafford, to defend the Puritans from Laud, to abolish
the Star Chamber and High Commission. So far the
House spoke with a single voice; but the deep-rooted
distrust of the King gradually led to the conviction
that nothing short of the transference of control to the
House of Commons could secure the ground that had
been won. Its resolve to accept dissolution at no hands
but its own was a measure of ordinary prudence.
Knowing that the King had only accepted the changes
under constraint, the majority adopted Pym's advice
to assume the executive power. The Grand Remon-
strance virtually proposed constitutional monarchy,
and no king of that age could be expected to surrender
his power without a struggle. The attempt on the Five
Members led to a demand for the control of the militia,
the rejection of which was followed by the refusal to
open the gates of Hull to the King. The Parliamentary
leaders were now no longer the champions of law and
precedent, for their claims were even more novel than
the unbridled prerogative against which they fought.
But to Charles belonged the main responsibility for
bringing things to such a pass.

As the struggle for power became keener it was
inevitable that certain champions of Parliament should
begin to ask themselves whether a king was really
necessary. In conversation with Hyde in 1641 Henry
Marten remarked that in his opinion one was not wise
enough to govern all—'the first word I ever heard man
speak to that purpose', adds the historian in recording

the incident. But this attitude was very rare, and when the same speaker declared in Parliament in 1643, 'Better one family be destroyed than many', he was sent to the Tower and excluded from his seat for two years. The Presbyterians, who had obtained control of the machine, were content with a narrowly limited monarchy; but when the royalist cause was crushed in the field by the New Model Army, the Independents became the dominant power in the State, and the abolition of the throne began to be freely discussed. The thirty-four votes cast in 1647 for Marten's proposal that no more addresses should be sent to the King measured the strength of the 'Commonwealth party', whose convictions and activities are recorded in Ludlow's vivid Memoirs. The conflict, however, was no longer between King and Parliament, but between Parliament and the Army.

The political history of the Army begins in 1647. 'They thought', relates Baxter, 'that God's providence had cast the trust of religion and the kingdom upon them as conquerors'; and the proposal of disbandment led to an explosion. While the officers formed a Council, the private soldiers chose agents or agitators, the two bodies quickly coalescing into the General Council of the Army, which pledged itself not to dissolve till it had obtained securities for the future. 'We are not a mere mercenary army', they declared, 'but called forth to the defence of our own and the people's just rights and liberties.' After abortive negotiations the troops occupied London and drove out the Presbyterian leaders. So far the Army was united; but a rift now began. The 'Heads of the Proposals', mainly the work of Ireton, failed to satisfy the rank and file. The agitators and some of the petty officers were much

E

more democratic than their leaders, whom they accused of lukewarmness in defending the rights of the people. The forward party in the Army now began to co-operate with the democrats outside, who asserted that the country should be governed neither by Parliament nor the Army, but by the people themselves. The name of Levellers appears to have owed its currency to Charles or to Cromwell. ' 'Twas their devilish intention', writes the royalist Heath, 'to abrogate and abolish the laws, to invade all property and by a wild parity to lay all things in common.' Even Clarendon affected to believe that they preached equality of estates. Edwards the Presbyterian declared Lilburne to resemble the Anabaptist John of Leyden 'as if he had been spit out of his mouth'. Prynne credited them with a desire for the total abrogation of the laws. The new party, however, stoutly repudiated such accusations, declaring that they were Levellers only so far as they were against every kind of tyranny. 'Equal justice to be impartially distributed to all, this is the levelling aimed at.' Their disclaimer of revolutionary principles was perfectly sincere, for they were neither socialists nor communists, but the earliest of British radicals.

John Lilburne, their leader, had been one of the Nonconformist victims of the Star Chamber, and had suffered exile in Holland. On the outbreak of war he entered the Army, rose to the rank of Lieutenant-Colonel, and was taken prisoner. At his trial he refused to plead to the indictment, maintaining that he had not taken arms against the King. His political philosophy developed rapidly under the stress of personal experiences. His attack on the Earl of Manchester having caused his committal by the Lords, he was led to insist on the sovereignty of the Commons. But, on being imprisoned by the Lower House for an attack on the King, he coolly transferred sovereignty to the nation at large. The conclusions which he had now reached and from which he never departed were set forth in the pamphlets issued during his imprisonment in Newgate in 1645. To maintain that Parliament was more considerable than the body it served was to say that an ambassador had more power than the prince by whom he was sent.

Such was the idea—the sovereignty of the common people—which spread like a conflagration through the Army when the fighting was over and the soldiers had leisure to reflect. The democratic teachings of Lilburne were also welcomed by a good many officers who scented the approaching struggle with Parliament and rejoiced to see its authority undermined. But the debates in the Army Council quickly revealed fundamental differences between the leaders and the rank and file. When the air was thick with rumours of accommodation with the King, the Levellers within and without the Army set forth their demands for manhood suffrage, equal electoral divisions and biennial Parliaments in *The Agreement of the People*. The exordium declares that the purpose of the proposals is to prevent another war or a relapse into slavery. The authority of Parliament was to be inferior only to those who chose it, and certain 'native rights', such as freedom of religion and equality before the law, were beyond its competence to assail. *The Case of the Army*, appearing almost simultaneously, added a few more specific demands. Monopolies and sinecures were to be abolished, the law to be codified, usurped privileges, such as enclosed common lands, to be restored.

When these documents were presented to the Commons they were at once pronounced destructive of the authority of Parliament and of the very foundation of government. In the Army Council, on the other hand, prolonged debates ensued, the reports of which by Clarke, the secretary, enable us to reconstruct the atmosphere with startling vividness. When Ireton attacked the demand for universal suffrage, the Levellers maintained that no man was bound to a government under which he had not put himself. For a vote it was not necessary to possess property; the reason which God had given to all was sufficient qualification. Even the poor had a birthright. Would it not be unjust if they had fought all this time for nothing? The 'Heads of Proposals' had admitted a Monarchy and a House of Lords and given them the joint control of the militia. Instead of 'laying the foundation of freedom for all manner of the people', the foundation of slavery was riveted more strongly than before. After prolonged debate, the 'Heads of Proposals' were reaffirmed, though the Levellers obtained an extension of the franchise to all who were not servants or beggars. But though the radicals forced their plan of manhood suffrage through the Council, it was of no avail, since Cromwell and Ireton remained invincibly opposed to its adoption. For a time the Levellers believed that the officers were intriguing with the King; but early in 1648 confidence was restored. The harmony, however, was brief. A number of Levellers were expelled from the Army, and representatives of the soldiers were no longer admitted to the Army Council. In an effective pamphlet the question was put which half England was asking itself: 'We were ruled before by King, Lords and Commons, now by a General, Court Martial and Commons; and we pray you what is the difference?' With the suppression of some petty mutinies the campaign of the Army Levellers comes to an end.

The civilians, on the other hand, led by Lilburne, pursued their way undaunted. After the death of Charles they asked for annual Parliaments, the abolition of tithes and imprisonment for debt. Work and a comfortable maintenance should be provided for the poor and impotent. The *Agreement of the People* was revised and described as 'the end and full scope of all our desires and intentions in government, wherein we shall rest absolutely satisfied'. They add that it should 'satisfy all ingenuous people that we are not such wild, irrational and dangerous creatures as we are aspersed'. Parliament was to consist of 400 members chosen by natural right by all of the age of twenty-one who are not servants nor in receipt of relief. No office-holder might be a member, and no member might sit in two successive Parliaments. Parliament might not legislate in matters of religion, grant monopolies, or impose taxes on food. In the judicial sphere the demand is for equality before the law, definite penalties, and the abolition of imprisonment for debt. Prisoners should be allowed counsel, all cases be settled within six months, tithes be abolished, and each parish might make its own arrangements with Ministers as to terms and salary. All public officers are to be elected locally, and to hold office for one year only. The Agreement was incapable of being altered by any Parliament, and an attempt to alter it was punishable by death.

Such was the most elaborate scheme of national reconstruction yet drawn up; but Lilburne's influence was due rather to his opposition to successful governments than to his charter of reform. A violent attack on Cromwell and Ireton in 1649 was followed by a trial, and his vigorous speech and acquittal created such an impression that a medal was struck to commemorate it. He was banished in 1652, but returned on the expulsion of the Rump, only to be re-arrested. His second trial created even more interest than the first. Twenty citizens offered bail of £2,000 each. To a judge's remark that he would be executed he replied that it would be the bloodiest day England had ever seen. During the trial three regiments stood under arms. Lilburne defended himself with his usual dexterity, and his acquittal raised his fame higher than ever. Cromwell, comments Clarendon, looked on it as a greater defeat than the loss of a battle. Again banished to Jersey, he was permitted to return in 1657 and died a Quaker a few days before his great enemy, the Protector. Other members of the party became involved in royalist intrigues, and with the death of its leader it fades out of history.

With far more truth than any other body of men during the Interregnum the Levellers could claim to be considered the people's party. While others placed sovereignty in King or Parliament, the Army, or the law, they proclaimed that it rested with the people alone. They appealed freely to the constitutional rights inherited from their ancestors; but they based their philosophy, not on precedent, but on the law of nature. Liberty, they believed, was not only guaranteed by a primeval contract, but was a right inherent in the very nature of human beings. By liberty they understood not merely freedom from the restraint of others, but a definite participation in whatever political arrangements the community found it desirable to make.

From this right of the individual to a share in power and responsibility springs the sovereignty of the people. It is not surprising that such doctrine appealed forcibly to humble citizens who saw one form of government follow another, all equally arbitrary in their dealings with public and private liberties. Such an appeal to an unwritten law, however, as Ireton pointed out, was in its essence anarchic. Valuable as an inspiration, it could not be taken as a rule of life, for everyone placed his own interpretation upon the oracle. In the second place, Lilburne credited the human unit with more wisdom than he possessed. The 'natural aristocracy' which, as Harrington was to maintain, is the life-blood of successful democratic government, finds no place in the system. He believed scarcely less in the equal capacity than in the equal rights of men; and he must be classed rather with the doctrinaires than with the statesmen of his age.

II

The strongest and most original thinker in the Army was Ireton, whose character and ideas were long misunderstood. 'This Cassius', declared Burnet, 'hoped all would become irreconcilable to monarchy, and stuck at nothing that would have turned England into a Commonwealth.' Sir Philip Warwick records the legend of the dying man's last words, 'I will have more blood'. The Clarke Papers have at last removed the veil which partially hid the Commissary General. Before their publication it was possible to denounce the insertion of a monarchical element in the 'Heads of Proposals' by a convinced republican. We now know that his proposals to the King merely embodied his speeches in the Army Council. Possessed of a larger stock of legal knowledge than his fellow officers and greater skill in putting his ideas into shape, Ireton was described by Lilburne as the Alpha and Omega of the Army. Whitelocke noticed that none could prevail with Oliver so much nor order him so far. A third observer remarks that Cromwell only shot the bolts that were hammered in Ireton's forge.

The 'Heads of Proposals', issued in the summer of 1647, show that the opinions of Ireton were by no means revolutionary. He is prepared for a fresh trial of government by King, Lords and Commons, with securities against the renewal of despotism. Biennial Parliaments were to sit from four to eight months every year, and the members to be elected by equal electoral districts. The militia was to be controlled by Parliament for ten years, and new peers must obtain the permission of the Commons to take their seats. The civil power of the Church was to be abolished, but the Covenant no longer to be imposed. 'Ireton', wrote his kinswoman, Mrs. Hutchinson, 'was not so fully of the opinion as his father-in-law (till he tried it and found the contrary), but that the King might have managed to comply with the public good of his people.' Though nobody who transferred sovereignty so decisively to the Commons or the Army can be called a constitutionalist, Ireton may be described as the leader of the constitutional party in the Army. So long as monarchy could be preserved, he was anxious to preserve it. 'We ought to keep to the constitution we have', he declared in argument with the Levellers, 'because it is the most fundamental and because there is so much reason, justice and prudence in it that I dare undertake there are many more evils that will follow in case you do alter than in the standing of it.'

In like manner Ireton vigorously attacked the doctrine of natural rights. In discussing the franchise he was led to explain his theory of property. Neither the hand of God nor the Law of Nature gave man property, which was of human institution. Sexby, the Leveller, hereupon cried out that the soldiers had ventured their lives to recover their birthrights, but, if he were right, they had none. Ireton replied that other birthrights than the use of air, the freedom of the highways and the fundamental part of the constitution had no existence. If civil law could be overridden at any moment by an appeal to the Law of Nature or to birthrights, no security would remain. 'When I hear of men's laying aside all engagements for some wild notion of what in every man's conception is just or unjust, I tremble at the boundless consequences.' The sole foundation of rights was the law of the land. To the plea that no man was bound to a government under which he had not placed himself he rejoined that men must obey the laws, whether they had assented to them or not. If they were dissatisfied, they could leave the country.

Ireton's politics were purely empirical. 'It is not to me so much as the vainest or lightest thing you can imagine', said he to the Levellers, 'whether there be a king in England or not.' He surrendered the form of the constitution when it could no longer be upheld, and so far yielded to the Army radicals as to allow the franchise to all who had directly assisted the Army against the King. But his distaste for popular demands remained unchanged. 'Men as men', said he, 'are corrupt and will be so'; and, like all who shared Hobbes's view of human nature and therefore of the primitive condition of mankind, he traces the origin of society solely to the necessity of securing order. 'That which leads all men into civil agreements and contracts and to make commonwealths is the necessity to preserve peace.' For this reason the sphere of the magistrate is confined to no special department, but extends over the whole range of life. When the Levellers, reinforced by several Independent ministers who had been invited to the discussion, insisted that his power should stop short of matters of religion, he offered the most strenuous opposition. There were too many things, he declared, which men might practise under pretence of religion. Human nature would require strong government as long as it remained unchanged. 'I am confident it is not the hand of man that will take away the power of monarchy in the earth', wrote Ireton, comprehending under that term all forms of strong government; 'if ever it be destroyed it will be by the breaking forth of the power of God amongst men to make such forms needless.' Had he lived two years longer he would have witnessed the rise to supreme power of the friend who was at once his military superior and his political pupil.

The publication of the Clarke Papers has at last rendered it possible to reconstruct the evolution of Cromwell's philosophy and to recognize the conservative stamp of his mind. 'I am very often judged for one that goes too fast', said he during the discussion in 1647 whether the Army should march to London and threaten Parliament. 'Give me leave to say this to you. What you have by force I look upon it as nothing.' The moderation in face of the exasperating conduct of Parliament found its counterpart in his attitude towards the Levellers. He was staggered by the number and magnitude of the changes foreshadowed in the *Agreement of the People*. 'Truly this paper does contain in it very great alterations of the government of the kingdom that it hath been under almost since it was a nation. How do we know if, whilst we are disputing about these things, another company of men shall gather together and put out a paper as plausible as this? And not only another but many of this kind? Would it not be utter confusion?' He bluntly rejected the proposal for universal suffrage. 'The consequences of this rule tend to anarchy. For where is there any bound or limit set if men that have but the interest of breathing shall have voices in elections?' His attitude to monarchy is equally moderate. He was only prepared to part with it if convinced that there was no alternative. He risked his popularity with the Army in his endeavour to arrive at a settlement, and earned the title of 'the King-ridden' from the eager republican, Henry Marten.

After the second civil war Oliver unburdened himself in a striking letter to Hammond. 'Authorities and powers are the ordinances of God; but all agree there are cases in which it is lawful to resist. The query is whether ours be such a case. My dear friend, let us look into providences; surely they mean somewhat. They hang so together; they have been so constant, clear, unclouded. Malice, swollen malice against God's people now called saints; and yet they, these poor saints, getting arms and therein blessed more and more.' He consented with reluctance to the King's execution; but Burnet relates that when the Scottish Commissioners came to beg for the King's life, Oliver 'entered into a lively discourse of the nature of the royal prerogative according to the principles of Mariana and Buchanan'. A year later he wrote that they had turned out a tyrant in a manner which all tyrants in the world would look at with fear, while many thousands of saints in England rejoiced to think of it.

After the death of the King, and still more after the Irish and Scottish victories, an ever-increasing number looked to Oliver to redress the evils under which the country was suffering; but there is no sign that till now he had ever thought of becoming supreme. After the Battle of Worcester, however, he invited several Members of Parliament to a meeting, and told them that, the King being dead and his son defeated, it was necessary to make some settlement. 'My meaning', said he, 'is that we should consider whether a republic or a mixed monarchical government will be best; and if something monarchical, then in whom power shall be placed.' After the discussion he remarked, 'I think a settlement of somewhat with monarchical power in it would be very effectual'. The debate proved that while the soldiers were one and all republican, the lawyers preferred some form of monarchy. After keeping silence for a year, Cromwell returned to the problem in 1652 in a conversation with Whitelocke. 'There is very great need for us', he began, 'to improve the mercies and successes God hath given us and not to be fooled out of them by our jarrings and animosities.' The Army, he continued, had conceived a strong dislike for Parliament. 'And I wish there were not too much cause for it. For really their pride and ambition and self-seeking do give too much ground for people to open their mouths. Unless there be some authority so full and so high as to keep things in better order, it will be impossible to prevent our ruin.' How could they be restrained, asked Whitelocke, since Parliament had been acknowledged as the supreme power? To which Cromwell replied by another question, 'What if a man should take upon him to be King?' After Whitelocke had remonstrated he continued, 'Surely the power of a king is so great and high and so universally understood and reverenced by the people of this nation that it would be of great advantage in such times as these'. Six months later the Rump was expelled and the Protectorate began.

Oliver had been stirred to action by learning that the Commons were forcing through a Bill to perpetuate their power. 'We could not believe such persons would be so unworthy', he remarked in his first speech after the event. 'We should have had a Council of State and a Parliament executing arbitrary government without intermission.' In every government, he added, there must be something unalterable, like a Magna Charta. 'That Parliaments should not make themselves perpetual is a fundamental. Liberty of conscience is a fundamental. That the command of the militia should be so placed that no one party in or out of Parliament have a power of ordering it is a fundamental.' But Parliament could not be trusted to preserve the fundamentals, and a single person must be at hand in times of crisis to protect the people. He defined his position as that of a police constable. To remove the apprehension that he might abuse his power he declared that he would not accept hereditary right for his family if it was offered.

Oliver soon found that to direct the destinies of a great nation was beyond the powers of a single man, and his second speech expressed his wish for a free Parliament. But such a body could only consist of worthy men who had opposed the King and possessed property. The new Parliament, however, did not inspire him with confidence, and he begged advice in all quarters, even among royalists. The strong man was acutely sensitive to criticisms from his old comrades. 'I know it is a trouble to my Lord', wrote Thurloe to Monk, 'to have any who is a saint in truth to be grieved or unsatisfied with him.' He longed to settle the Government on a more constitutional basis. When a pamphleteer maintained that possession was the only right to power, he ordered the book to be burnt. His wish to assume the royal title arose not from contempt but from respect for legality. He told Parliament that he would rather have any name from it than any name without it. The same resolution to change as little as possible appears in his relations with the Church. The expulsion of incumbents he found for the most part consummated; but such as had escaped he allowed to remain. Anglican services were held publicly, and the sermons of Fuller and other divines in the metropolis were thronged. Ussher had his library restored to him, and was told that all restraints would be removed from the Episcopalians if they would leave politics alone. He intervened to protect individuals and sects in danger of persecution, and allowed the Jews to return to England. His desire was to govern justly, moderately, and constitutionally, and it was the fault of circumstance that he was forced to rule as an autocrat.

CHAPTER V

MILTON AND HARRINGTON

I

THE foremost English man of letters of the seventeenth century was also a great patriot, who entered into the problems and trials of his country with every fibre of his being. During the twenty crowded years which followed the meeting of the Long Parliament the author of *L'Allegro* and *Il Penseroso*, *Comus* and *Lycidas* laid aside his lyre and plunged headlong into the controversies, political and ecclesiastical, by which England was torn. His first campaign was waged against episcopacy in the person of its champion, Bishop Hall, and the five pamphlets which followed each other in rapid succession displayed the lofty eloquence and the vehement passion which were to adorn and disfigure all his prose works. At this stage he leaned to Presbyterianism; but the ascendancy of the sect soon taught him that New Presbyter was but Old Priest writ large.

A stringent decree for the control of printers and booksellers, issued in 1637 and neglected during the years of civil strife, was virtually reproduced in 1643 by an ordinance of the Lords and Commons. Milton sat down to prepare a protest, and the *Areopagitica*, cast in the form of a speech to Parliament, appeared in 1644. The exordium stoutly defends the right of free comment, on the ground that it is at once a privilege of citizenship and a benefit to the State. He proceeds to lodge an emphatic protest against the war on books. 'For they are not absolutely dead things, but do contain a potency of life in them to be as active as that soul whose progeny they are. As good almost kill a man as kill a good book. Who kills a man kills a reasonable creature; but he who destroys a book kills reason itself, the image of God. Many a man lives a burden to the earth; but a good book is the precious life-blood of a master spirit, embalmed and treasured up on purpose to a life beyond life.' Frankly admitting that there is evil in many books, he refuses to praise 'a fugitive and cloistered virtue that never sallies out and sees her adversary'. A wise man, like a good refiner, can gather gold out of dross, and will make better use of an old pamphlet than a fool of Scripture. When God gave man reason, He gave him freedom to choose, and reason is but choosing. That the censorship blighted whatever it touched was brought home to the author in Italy, where 'nothing had been written these many years but flattery and fustian. There it was that I found and visited the famous Galileo grown old, a prisoner to the Inquisition, for thinking in astronomy otherwise than the Franciscan and Dominican licensers'. England, though not cursed with the Inquisition, was then groaning under the prelatical yoke, and he dared not at that time hope that 'those worthies were then breathing in her air who should be her leaders to such a deliverance as shall never be forgotten by any revolution of time'. When the era of emancipation arrived he never dreamed that he would have to listen at home to the same complaints that he had heard among learned men abroad. Bishop and Presbyter, it was becoming plain, were equally committed to the thraldom of learning.

Our faith and knowledge, continues Milton, thrive by exercise, like our limbs. 'The light which we have gained was given us not to be ever staring on, but by it to discover onward things more remote from our knowledge.' If a man believes things because his pastor says so or the Assembly so determines, 'though his belief be true, yet the very truth he holds becomes his heresy'. A policy of coercion was unworthy of the country and the time. 'Lords and Commons of England, consider what nation it is whereof ye are the governors—a nation not slow and dull, but of a quick, ingenious and piercing spirit, acute to invent, subtle and sinewy to discourse, not beneath the reach of the highest that human capacity can soar to. What wants there to such a pregnant soil but wise and faithful labourers to make a nation of prophets, of sages and of worthies? Methinks I see in my mind a noble and puissant nation rousing herself like a strong man after sleep, and shaking her invincible locks. Methinks I see her as an eagle renewing her mighty youth and kindling her undazzled eyes at the fuller midday beam; purging and unscaling her long-abused sight at the fountain itself of heavenly radiance, while the timorous birds and those that love the twilight flutter about amazed at what she means. Should ye then suppress all this flowery crop of knowledge and bring a famine in our minds again?'

After this imperishable tribute to his countrymen Milton concludes with a soaring panegyric on truth. 'Truth is strong, next to the Almighty. She needs no policies, nor stratagems nor licensings to make her victorious. Who ever knew Truth put to the worse in a free and open encounter?' After this impassioned vindication of liberty it is a shock to discover that he excludes from toleration 'popery and open superstition which, as it extirpates all religious and civil suprem-

acies, so itself should be extirpate, provided first that
all charitable and compassionate means be used to win
and regain the weak and misled'. In Catholicism he
saw not a set of dogmas, but a gigantic engine of
persecution and oppression, and in the name of
liberty he refused it liberty. In the province of
religious toleration Milton was behind many of his
contemporaries. Yet the whole spirit of the treatise is
against exceptions, and its piercing cry, 'Give me
liberty to know, to utter and to argue freely according
to conscience above all liberties', rings through the
centuries.

If the plea for unlicensed printing was at worst
a paradox to most of his contemporaries, the treatises
on divorce, the bitter wail of a disillusioned husband,
created open scandal even in an age when men were
drifting far from their moorings. Thus, when he at
length came forward as a political teacher, Milton was
already widely regarded as a libertine who would be
tied by no obligation to God or man. *The Tenure of
Kings and Magistrates*, published a fortnight after the
tragic scene outside Whitehall, was a bold announcement that he identified himself with the regicides.
Aubrey remarks that the roots of his republicanism lay
in his 'being so conversant in Livy and the Roman
authors and the greatness he saw done by the Roman
Commonwealth'; and his satisfaction at the result of
the Second Civil War was recorded in the sonnet to
Fairfax on the siege of Colchester. But though he
confesses that he would have been ready to have signed
the death-warrant, there is nothing to denote that he
preferred a republic to any other form of government,
and he was still able to conceive of a king who should
not be a tyrant. Men were born free, he declares, in

the image of God; but wrong and violence entering in from Adam's sin, they contracted to bind each other from mutual injury. One or more individuals were entrusted with the administration of the affairs of the community, not as lords but as commissioners. The power remained in the people, and it could not be taken from them without a violation of their birthright. To affirm that kings are accountable to God alone overturned all law; for if they feared not God—and most do not—the people held their lives and estates by a precarious tenure. The people may therefore reject and depose them whenever they like, by the right of freeborn men to be governed in accordance with their wishes. And if it is within their discretion to depose a good king, it is a sacred duty to depose a tyrant. If the law of nature allows a man to defend himself even against the king in person, does it not still more justify the self-defence of a commonwealth? Honour, then, to those who dared to teach the world that 'for the future no potentate, but to his sorrow, may presume to turn upside down whole kingdoms of men.'

The *Eikon Basilike*, or King's Book, a clever forgery by Gauden, a royalist divine, appeared almost at the same time as *The Tenure of Kings and Magistrates*, and, rising on the crest of a great wave of reaction, appeared to the Council of State sufficiently formidable to demand an answer. The task was entrusted to Milton, who had been appointed Latin Secretary on the publication of his defence of regicide. The reply came in the autumn of 1649 in the fiery pages of the *Eikonoklastes*. The work follows the monarch, 'or his household rhetorician', step by step through the events of the long struggle. There is a new bitterness in these pages—in the credulity with which he accepts the legend of the King's murder of his father and his connexion with the Irish massacres, in his unfeeling jeer at Charles's vain request for his chaplains. The attitude towards monarchy itself has also changed. 'We learn from both sacred and profane history', he remarks aggressively, 'that the kings of this world have ever hated and instinctively feared the Church of God.' Kings, though strong in legions, are weak in argument; 'since they have ever been accustomed from their cradle to use their will only as their right hand, their reason as their left'. A still more remarkable modification of his thought has taken place. Opinion had been gravely shocked, not in royalist circles alone, by the death of the King, and the tide was already beginning to set strongly towards a Restoration. It flashed on Milton that he had over-estimated the wisdom and worth of the mass of individuals who composed the nation. The country of free men, each with his instinct for liberty and his divine origin, has given place to 'an inconstant, irrational and hapless herd, begotten to servility', hypnotised by the childish device of the King at his prayers. We are already moving towards the aristocratic republicanism which most nearly reflects the poet's austere temperament.

The execution of Charles was an event in European as well as in English history, and the champions of the monarchical principle loudly expressed their horror. The most formidable onslaught came from Salmasius, Professor at Leyden, who at the request of Charles II, then at the Hague, composed his *Defensio Regia pro Carolo I*, and whose commanding position among European scholars procured wide currency for his writings. Milton alone was fitted by his fame and his command of Latin to vindicate his country in the eyes

of the world, and at the invitation of the Council of
State he accepted the challenge. His labours on the
manifesto cost him his eyes, a sacrifice proudly
recorded in one of the noblest of his sonnets. In the
Defensio Populi Anglicani there is much of the scurrilous
vituperation in which even the most cultured controversialists of the seventeenth century rejoiced; but
there is also brilliant and vigorous writing. 'You liken
a monarchy to the government of the world by one
God. I pray you, answer me whether you think any
can deserve to be invested with a power here on earth
that shall resemble His power, except such a person
as doth infinitely excel all other men?' When his
opponent appeals to the Law of Nature, Milton gladly
joins issue on that ground. It is easy to prove that
nothing is more agreeable to the Law of Nature than
that punishment should be inflicted on tyrants; for it
is a principle imprinted on all men's minds to regard
the good of mankind. No king can pretend any right
to do mischief. Hereditary rule, again, is contrary to
the Law of Nature; for nobody has a right to be king
unless he excels all others in wisdom and courage.
Nature appoints that wise men should govern fools,
not that the wicked should rule over the good; and
they who take the government out of such unworthy
hands act agreeably to natural law. It was of this
celebrated controversy, which aroused extraordinary
interest throughout Europe, that Hobbes wrote, 'They
are very good Latin both, and hardly to be judged
which is better; and both very ill reasoning, hardly
to be judged which is worse'.

Milton's reply to Salmasius described the government of the Commonwealth as being 'such as our
present distractions admit of, not such as could be

wished'. His *Second Defence of the English People*, published in 1654, expresses the affectionate admiration of the Puritan poet for the Puritan Protector. 'He has either extinguished or learnt to subdue the whole host of vain hopes, fears and passions which infest the soul.' Addressing Oliver directly, he proceeds, 'While you are left among us, that man has no proper trust in God who fears for the security of England. We all willingly yield the palm of sovereignty to your incomparable ability and virtue, except those few who, ambitious of honours they have not the power to sustain, envy those conferred on one more worthy than themselves, or who do not know that nothing is more pleasing to God or agreeable to reason than that the supreme power should be vested in the best and wisest.' No such belief in the wisdom of Parliaments existed in his mind as rendered the very conception of a Protectorate inconsistent with republicanism for men like Ludlow and Vane. Yet there are distinct indications that the rule of Cromwell seemed to him insufficiently national. 'Reflect often', he adjures the omnipotent Protector, 'what a dear pledge your land has committed to your care. That liberty she once expected from the chosen flower of her talents and virtues she now expects from you only, and through you alone hopes to obtain. If you, hitherto the tutelary genius of liberty, should hereafter invade it, the general interests of piety and virtue will be affected. In no other way can you render our liberty at once so ample and secure as by associating in your councils the companions of your dangers and toils.' His wishes extended beyond the broadening of the base of government. He had inserted a demand for disestablishment in the forefront of the sonnet to Cromwell. While religion was connected with civil magistracy the temple of liberty lacked its roof; and he became more and more convinced that the power to grant or withhold the rights of the people ought not to be in the hands of a single man, however disinterested and conscientious.

Unlike the Commonwealthsmen, Milton did not suggest that the edifice of liberty could be buttressed by Parliament. Nowhere in his former treatises do we find such derisive condemnation of the shibboleths of democracy. The individual had a birthright to freedom, not to power. 'Who would vindicate your right of unrestrained suffrage', he asks in almost savage tones, 'merely that you might elect the creatures of your own faction or him, however small might be his worth, who would give you the most lavish feasts and enable you to drink to the greatest excess? Ought the guidance of the republic to be entrusted to persons to whom nobody would entrust the management of their private concerns? Who would suppose he would ever be made a jot more free by such a crew of functionaries?' It was a sad position that Milton had reached. Despite his admiration for the Protector, he was secretly dissatisfied with the rule of a single person. Despite his belief in the sovereignty of the people, he had no faith in representative government.

The poet watched the approaching collapse of the Commonwealth with brooding indignation; and when the Restoration was in sight he launched his *Ready and Easy Way to establish a Free Commonwealth*. The pamphlet, published in February 1660, was the boldest and most passionate that he ever wrote. Kingship is unnecessary, burdensome and dangerous, and the government of a single person in any form is scouted.

'The people must needs be mad or strangely in-
fatuated that build the chief hope of their common
happiness and safety on a single person, who, if he
happen to be good, can be no more than another man,
and, if bad, hath in his hands to do more evil without
check.' The trade of a sovereign is to 'pageant himself
up and down among the perpetual bowings and cring-
ing of an abject people'. Passing to the political situation he cries aloud in poignant anguish. 'That a nation
should be so valorous to win their liberty in the field,
and when they have won it not know how to use it or
value it, but basely and besottedly run their necks
again into the yoke which they have broken and
prostrate all the fruits of their victory at the feet of the
vanquished, will be such an example as kings and
tyrants never yet had the like to boast of.' Once again
he appeals to a code higher than human laws. 'We are
not bound by any statute of preceding Parliaments, but
by the law of Nature only, which is the only law truly
and properly to all mankind fundamental.'

What had Milton to propose at this crisis of his
country's fate? He calmly assumes that 'all ingenuous
and knowing men' agree with him that a free Commonwealth without Single Person or House of Lords is by
far the best government. True they had never reached
it; but it might now be established for ever without
difficulty or delay. If the people, laying aside their
prejudices and considering their own good, elected
suitable knights and burgesses, the work would be
done. At this point our publicist produces a startling
novelty. The Grand Council is to be perpetual. The
ship is always under sail; if those who sit at the stern
steer well, why change them? 'How can we be ad-
vantaged by successive and transitory Parliaments?

If they find no work to do, they will make it.' It occurs to him, however, that permanence might not be tolerated. 'If the ambition of such as think themselves injured that they do not partake of the government cannot brook a perpetuity of others chosen before them, or if it be feared that long continuance of power may corrupt the sincerest men, there is the expedient, lately propounded, that annually the third part of the senators may go out.' But this qualification is allowed with a bad grace. The wheel is too much like the wheel of fortune. It is idle to expect anything from a floating foundation, and the safest course is that none shall be removed but on conviction of crime.

Milton's last great pamphlet is the supreme condemnation of the political thinker. The noblest champion of liberty to which the age gave birth pleaded for a yoke heavier than that against which he had fought so zealously. We are tempted to quote the author of the *Areopagitica* against himself. 'To sequester ourselves out of the world into Utopian politics which cannot be drawn into use will never mend our condition.' 'Can one read it', asked John Adams more than a century later, 'without shuddering? An assembly of senators for life? If no better system of government was proposed, no wonder the people recalled the Royal Family.' The pamphlet is, however, not inexplicable. In the early days of the struggle he had seen a mighty and puissant nation awaking as a man out of sleep. The triumph of freedom in England had appeared to him an event of universal significance. 'I behold all the nations of the earth', he wrote in 1654, 'recovering that liberty they so long had lost; I behold them spreading the blessings of freedom and civilization among the kingdoms of the world.' It was the contrast between the unique opportunity for the race to step forward towards a higher civilization and the unripeness of his fellow men that drove him into the despairing paradox of a perpetual senate. Milton was a prophet, not a philosopher. No one has ever loved liberty with a nobler and more unselfish passion; but few political teachers have so little understood how it was to be obtained and defended.

II

James Harrington, the author of *Oceana*, entered the service of Charles I as Gentleman of the Bedchamber. 'Finding him to be an ingenious man', writes Wood, 'his Majesty loved his company, and did choose rather to discourse with him than with the others of his chamber. They had often discussions concerning government; but when they happened to talk of a Commonwealth, the King seemed not to endure it.' The man who talked of Commonwealths with the King in the dreary days of his captivity, yet won his love and gave his own in return, is a figure of peculiar interest and fascination. Born of good family in 1611, he supplemented his residence at Oxford by prolonged travels on the Continent, mixing with the Courts and Cabinets of half a dozen countries, and studying their language, literature, and institutions. He used to say in later life that before he left England he knew of monarchy and aristocracy, democracy and oligarchy, only as hard words to be looked for in a dictionary. After visits to the Netherlands, Denmark and France, he passed into Italy, where the true political schooling of his life was to begin, taking up his station for the greater part of the time at Venice.

What gives such peculiar importance to his observation of the Venetian system is not only that he was its first genuine student, but that he alone of the distinguished thinkers of the time derived many of his proposals from it.

Harrington returned to England a convinced Republican, and his opinions prevented him from throwing in his lot unreservedly with any party in the great struggle which soon burst over the land. In 1647, however, he accepted a post under the captive monarch. Finding the King 'quite another person than he had been represented to him, he became passionately affected with him and took all occasion to vindicate him in what company soever he might be'. The story of their political discussions went abroad, and dutiful royalists testified that the King had worsted him in an argument. Possessing the confidence of both sides, he naturally used his influence to procure a compromise, though his principles remained wholly unaffected. But his interventions on his master's behalf were misunderstood, and he was removed from his post. The friendship of the Republican and the champion of Divine Right does equal credit to both. They never met again, and Aubrey often heard Harrington say that 'nothing ever went more near to him than the death of the King'.

When the monarchy was gone, he set to work on the political system which has immortalized his name. We do not need the charming story of Lady Claypole's interposition with her father for the 'stolen child' to make us believe that *Oceana*, which appeared in 1656, was the pride of its author's heart. It is, indeed, the complete exposition of the completed system. It lacks the magic of style, and has therefore joined the great army of books which are often mentioned and seldom read. We miss the thunderous roll of Milton's prose, the pregnant brevity of Hobbes, the scintillating aphorisms of Halifax; yet Harrington is more original than any of them.

He begins by pointing out that the true principle by which governments should be estimated is that of the balance of forces, a discovery made by the founders of the Venetian Commonwealth. The perfection of government is to be found where the sovereignty is not limited, but 'librated'. At first sight it might seem that this brings us to the familiar expedient of mixed government. But the resemblance is merely in the bare fact of the division of power. All power in a state is of two sorts, external and internal, deriving from wealth on the one hand and from intellectual distinction on the other. It is the function of the material power to guarantee equality in the foundation, of the intellectual to secure freshness in the super-structure.

But how are these results to be achieved? Harrington's capital contribution to political thinking was to show that the distribution of power must in the long run correspond to the distribution of property. To this conclusion he was led partly by his studies of Roman history, partly by the experiences of his own country. Since the accession of Henry VII, he declared, land had been passing in ever-increasing quantities from the nobility to the people, and power must follow it. The tendency towards the break-up of great estates was to be accelerated by an agrarian law limiting the quantity of land to be held by an individual to the value of £2000 a year, and also by the division of property among all the children. Though he thought and wrote in terms of land, he realized that in commercial communities such as Holland or Genoa power would follow the distribution of capital. He was the first of modern thinkers to recognize the decisive influence of economic phenomena on political structure and function.

In the next place, the freshness of life by which the State makes progress is effected by rotation. Rotation ensures that, as the blood of the body circulates and is prevented from becoming stagnant by being pumped through the heart, the individual members of the community take their share in the government of the commonwealth. Since its full advantages are only to be enjoyed where the suffrages of the people really express their will, it is necessary that this freedom of pronouncement be secured by the ballot. Bearing these principles in mind, the construction of the machine of government becomes easy. Take any twenty men, and a difference will at once reveal itself. Six will at any rate be less foolish than the rest, and these will lead. In other words, a 'natural aristocracy' is diffused throughout the whole body of mankind. The duty of its members is to be counsellors of the people, their task to debate and advise. If they could do more, the government would not be equal; consequently there must be another council to decide. As the senate would represent the wisdom of the community, which lies in the aristocracy, the assembly should represent its interest, which lies in the whole body of the people. The duty of the assembly is to accept or reject the proposals of the senate. The government, completed by the election of the magistracy, may be summed up as 'the senate proposing, the people resolving, the magistracy executing'.

True government resting on persuasion, weekly classes for the explanation of the constitution are to be held, and a thousand officials are to traverse the country to give the people their first lessons in the mysteries of the ballot, since all elections, local as well as general, are conducted on that principle. Even the Poet Laureate is to be elected by the popular vote. The essence of a commonwealth is equality. With an agrarian law in operation the nobility and gentry would no longer achieve their position in the State by riches, but by their education and their capacity for public service. When their intrinsic merit, weighed by the judgement of the people, was the only path to honour and preferment, the amassing of possessions would become a less prevalent ambition.

The religious life of the nation is under the control of a national council of religion. On the vacancy of a living, two representatives are to repair to one of the Universities—which should be prudently reformed— and petition the Vice-Chancellor and Convocation for a probationer. The candidate selected by the University returns to the parish and, after one year, the suffrages of the parishioners are taken by ballot. If two-thirds of the voters indicate their approval, the probationer enters on his duties as the recognized minister. That suitable candidates may be induced to enter the ministry every benefice in the nation shall be augmented to the value of £100 a year. That liberty of conscience may be secure, no coercive power may be exercised by any man or body of men. Religious liberty consists not simply in toleration, but in the total absence of disqualifications. Disputed questions are to be settled by the divines of the two Universities, debating and deciding independently of each other.

That the clergy may have no cause to neglect their duties they are ineligible for any other employment. In this way the freedom of the people and the supervision of the most learned members of the State are combined. No political writer has discerned with greater clearness the importance of education in the life and well-being of a State. A better system of instruction had been one of the petitions of Milton to the Protector in the *Defensio Secunda,* and a scheme had been outlined in the *Letter to Hartlib*; but Harrington came forward with practical proposals, anticipating in a very striking way the modern system of universal and compulsory education under the control of the State.

Harrington's selection of an imaginary setting for his ideas was dictated by the rigorous censorship of the Protectorate. His political works were no mere speculative pastime, but an earnest and practical exhortation to his countrymen. *Oceana* is the least Utopian of Utopias, and is one of the earliest examples in political thinking of the historical method. 'No man', he thought, 'can be a politician except he be first a historian and a traveller. For if he has no knowledge in history, he cannot tell what has been; and if he is not a traveller, he cannot tell what is. But he that neither knows what has been nor what is can never tell what must be nor what may be.' Harrington himself, as his fellow attendant on the King records, was the 'best read man in history of all sorts' he had ever known. In the crisis of 1659 he prefaces his *Model of a Commonwealth fitted to the Present State of this Nation* by a sketch of seven of the principal republican constitutions of history. Though he stands fast by the notion of a right reason or natural law, every regulation in *Oceana* is judged at the bar of history before its adoption.

It would, however, be idle to deny that there are traces of the doctrinaire. As Pitt refused to suppress Godwin's *Political Justice* on the ground that a three-guinea book could do no harm, so Cromwell allowed *Oceana* to circulate on the ground that it was too unpractical to be dangerous. 'Our fierce champions of a free state', said L'Estrange with considerable truth, 'presuppose great unity, great probity, great purity.' Harrington supports the principle of rotation because he believes that there is an inexhaustible supply of worthy and capable men ready to play their part in the drama of government. He upholds the universality of the elective principle because, in the words of Baxter, he is convinced that men are wise enough to choose the wise and good enough to choose the good. He believes that the different organs of government will be satisfied with the functions allotted to them in the Constitution. 'In this Constitution', he announces confidently, 'the councils must of necessity contain the wisdom and interest of the nation.' But in his enthusiasm for certain results secured by the institutions of Sparta and Venice he forgets that liberty was almost lost in their meshes. As Hume was to point out, no sufficient security for freedom or for the redress of grievances was to be found in a scheme where the senate could negative a proposal before it ever reached the votes of the people.

In Harrington's pages there is none the less to be found a breadth of conception as remarkable as Milton's in combination with a genius for details that was his own. More clearly than any of his contemporaries he saw that a good government was an organism, and that it must grow naturally out of the social and economic conditions of society. He stands in the front rank of those thinkers who have combined democratic principles with the interests of order no less than of progress. The prophet was for a short time not without honour in his own country, and it is not difficult to believe the testimony of Anthony Wood that *Oceana* was greedily bought. Such interest did it arouse that the Rota Club, perhaps the first debating society in English history, was formed in 1659 for the discussion of its proposals. We are fortunate in possessing a spirited account of the proceedings of the famous club by Aubrey, who was one of its members. The doctrine, he informs us, was the more taking that there was at that time, to human foresight, no possibility of the King's return. The discourses themselves were the most smart and ingenious he had ever heard or expected to hear; indeed, the debates in Parliament were but flat beside them. The room was every evening as full as it could be crammed. A special attraction was found in the use of the balloting box, which was brought into requisition at the close of the debate. Pepys turned his steps thither more than once, and found a 'great confluence of gentlemen and admirable discourse'. Numerous tracts and broadsides published in the interval between the deposition of Richard Cromwell and the Declaration of Breda bear additional witness to the impression that Harrington's system had made on the public mind. For about a year his name was on every lip. But the nation had had enough of experiments, and Utopias, however plausible, were rejected in favour of the historic constitution of King, Lords, and Commons. The Restoration closed his career, and a period of

G

imprisonment partially unhinged his reason. Though he lived on for several years, he ceased to write, and his death passed unnoticed.

Harrington's wisdom, however, was not buried in his grave. Hume pronounced *Oceana* the only rational model of a commonwealth, and Coleridge ranked its author with Thucydides, Machiavelli, and Bacon. A manuscript essay in the British Museum reveals Grote's appreciation of the first great champion of the ballot. His writings were even more read and admired beyond the Atlantic. The Constitutions of Carolina, New Jersey, and Pennsylvania reflected his thought, and a century later his authority was freely quoted in the discussions which preceded and followed the elaboration of the American Constitution. His works formed the political bible of Otis and John Adams, and Jefferson's copy is preserved in the Library of Congress. Translated into French during the Revolution, they supplied Sieyès with many of his ideas. Thus Harrington's name arrests us in the three great revolutions of the modern world.

CHAPTER VI

WINSTANLEY AND THE COMMUNISTS

THOUGH the working-classes stood aloof from the great struggle, they shared the general expectation that the establishment of the Republic would usher in the era of reform. The rise of prices consequent on the discovery of new supplies of the precious metals had been followed but slowly by the increase of wages, and the hardship was heightened by the monopoly prices demanded for many of the necessaries of life. To these chronic evils was added, during the fifth decade of the century, a series of unusually bad harvests. The war, too, brought with it a large increase of taxation and the intolerable vexation of free quarter. Though the miserable condition of the poor was constantly discussed, the pamphlets and newspapers of the time are full of lament that no improvement was being effected.

The new doctrine of communism was outlined in a pamphlet published in December 1648. *The Light Shining in Buckinghamshire* announces in its sub-title a discussion of the main cause of the slavery of the world. By the grant of God all were free alike, and no individual was intended to exercise rule over his fellow-men. 'But man, following his sensuality, became an encloser, so that all the land was enclosed in a few mercenary hands and all the rest made their slaves.' Of these robbers the most desperate was made king in order to protect the rest in their mis-doings. Each should have a just portion, so that none need to beg nor steal for want. The government should be carried on by elders chosen by the people, who would decide all questions in every town and hamlet without further trouble. At the present time, however, we were governed by nobles and priests. Our nobility and gentry were originally the servants of William the Conqueror; their rise was their country's ruin, and their suppression would be the restoration of popular rights. 'The base priests preach all our powers and constitutions to be *Jure Divino*. Shake off these locusts and be no more deluded by them; cast off these abominable deceivers.'

Four months later, the exhortation 'To your tents, O Israel', with which the strange pamphlet had closed, bore fruit. On 16 April 1649 the Council of State received the following intelligence: 'On Sunday sennight last, there was one Everard, once of the army but cashiered, who termeth himself a prophet, and four more came to St. George's Hill in Surrey and began to dig, and sowed the ground with parsnips, carrots and beans. On Monday following they were there again, being increased in their number. On Friday they came again, twenty or thirty, and wrought all day at digging. They do threaten to pull down and level all park pales and lay open and intend to plant them. They give out that they will be four or five thousand within ten days, and threaten the neighbouring people they will make them all come up to the hills and work.' The letter was forwarded by Bradshaw to Fairfax, with a request that he should send some horse to disperse the disorderly gathering. A force was at once dispatched, and three days later Fairfax was informed that the affair was not worth notice. There had never been above twenty of the diggers. The following day Everard and Winstanley, the leaders, appeared before the Council of State and explained their conduct. All the liberties of the people, declared Everard, had been lost by the coming of the Conqueror. The time of deliverance was now at hand, and God would restore them their freedom to enjoy the fruits of the earth. A vision had appeared to him, and a voice had bid him dig and plough the earth and receive the fruits thereof. They did not intend to meddle with property nor to break any enclosures, but only to take what was common and untilled and to make it fruitful. They were willing to live in tents like their forefathers. The speaker had kept his hat on in the presence of the General, remarking that he was their fellow creature. No further steps were taken by the Government at the time. They felt, perhaps, that rumour had exaggerated the importance of the diggers, whom after Everard's speech they were inclined to regard as harmless fanatics. A week after the examination, however, appeared a manifesto revealing the fact that behind the artless confession to which they had listened lay a philosophy which threatened every existing institution.

The *True Levellers' Standard advanced, or the State of Community opened and presented to the Sons of Men* was a 'declaration to the powers of England and to the powers of the world why the common people had begun to dig on St. George's Hill'. 'In the beginning', runs the manifesto, 'the great creator Reason made the Earth a common treasury for beasts and man.' But man falling into blindness was brought into bondage, and became a greater slave to his own kind than the beasts of the field to him. The earth was bought and sold, and was hedged in by the rulers. For a certain time the creator, the spirit Reason, thus suffered himself to be rejected; whence arose wars to uphold dominion and riches. But when the earth again becomes a common treasury, as it must, for Reason and all the prophecies of Scripture point to it, enmity will cease; for none will desire a larger share than another. Passing from an exposition of their philosophy to a vindication of their conduct, the authors declare that they have met with resistance because they proclaim universal liberty, which was not only their birthright, but which they had bought with their money and blood in the war. All landlords lived in breach of the commandment 'Thou shalt not steal'. They had induced the plain-hearted poor to work for them with small wages, and by their work had made great fortunes. By their very labour the poor raised up tyrants to rule over them. It had been revealed to them in dreams where they should begin to dig, and though the earth might be barren they would receive a blessing from the spirit. 'You Pharaohs, you have rich clothing and full bellies, you have your honours and your ease; but know the day of judgement is begun and that it will reach you ere long. The poor people you oppress shall be the saviours of the land. If you will find mercy, let Israel go free; break to pieces the bands of property.'

The diggers still remained quietly employed at St. George's Hill. On his way from Guildford to London at the end of May Fairfax visited the locality and found twelve of them hard at work. To a short admonition from the General they replied that they were digging Crown lands, and that the king who possessed them by the Norman Conquest being dead, they reverted to the common people. The day after the visit of the General appeared another manifesto of the party, addressed to the Lords of Manors, who were cutting and selling trees on common lands. 'God has enlightened our hearts to see that the earth was not made purposely for you to be the lords and we to be your slaves.' But they still declared that they had no intention of resorting to force. This appeal producing no effect, a letter was dispatched to Fairfax. He had been mild and moderate to them in court and when he had come to see them, and the diggers were thereby emboldened to plead with him for justice. The laws that had been made in the days of monarchy had given freedom to the gentry and clergy, but had done nothing for the people.

In July Winstanley and two of his comrades were brought before the Court at Kingston for trespass, the jury consisting of 'such as stood strongly for the Norman power'. They were forbidden to speak and were heavily fined. They promptly dispatched an account of their arrest and sentence to the House of Commons, enclosing a list of some of the abominations which William the Conqueror introduced into England, among which were those of tithes and lawyers. In the autumn a more serious attack was made upon the little community, when a party of soldiers pulled down the two houses in which they were living and carried the wood away in a cart. A long and eloquent letter from Winstanley followed. Parliament had virtually said to them, 'Give us taxes, free quarter, excise, venture your lives with us to cast out the oppressor, and we will make you a free people.' They had agreed, the victory had been won, and the spoil should be equally divided. They claimed freedom in the common land by virtue of their conquest over the King, for they had bought it by their blood and money. If the Government denied them their request, it would have to raise money for their support; whereas, if they were allowed to reclaim the waste land, England would be enriched. It was a stain on a Christian nation that there should be so much waste land and that so many should starve for want. The destruction of the houses seems to have put an end to the little settlement. But the leader of the diggers was far from losing heart or bating a jot of his principles. In *A New Year's Gift for the Parliament and Army* he attempted to demonstrate that branches of kingly power still remained. Tithes had been promised to the clergy by the Conqueror on condition they would 'preach him up'. Our old law-books were still in use and should be burnt in Cheapside. If the government was to be new, let the laws be new also. For England was a prison; the subtleties of its laws the bolts and bars; the lawyers its jailers. 'At this very day poor people are forced to work for 4*d*. a day, and corn is dear. And the tithing-priest stops their mouth and tells them that "inward satisfaction of mind" was meant by the declaration "The poor shall inherit the earth". I tell you, the scripture is to be really and materially fulfilled. You jeer at the name Leveller. I tell you Jesus Christ is the head Leveller.'

Gerard Winstanley had gradually won his position as the acknowledged leader of the English Communists. He prefaces his *Watchword to the City of London* with a few lines of autobiography. 'I was once a freeman of thine, but beaten out of estate and trade by thy cheating sons in the thieving art of buying and selling. I was therefore forced to live a country life, where likewise with taxes and free quarter my weak back found the burden heavier than I could bear.' While his worldly prospects were at a low ebb he received consolation from an unexpected source. 'Not a year since, my heart was filled with sweet thoughts and many things were revealed to me I never read in books nor heard from the mouth of flesh. Then I took my spade and began to dig on St. George's Hill.' The experiment had been interrupted, and Winstanley now set himself to elaborate the constructive part of his system. In February 1652 appeared *The Law of Freedom*, with a dedication to 'All the Nations of the Earth'.

The Dedicatory Epistle informs Cromwell that he and his officers had not conquered by their unaided efforts, but by the help of the common people, whose right it was to share in the victory and whom a mere change of names would never satisfy. Tithes still swallowed up the savings of the poor. Even where the laws were good they were tampered with by magistrates. Worst of all, the landlords still ruled the country as tyrants. It might be asked how the clergy and the landowners were to exist if tithes and service were withdrawn. But in the new society there must be no buying nor selling, for with bargaining came deception and from deceit sprang oppression. With the disappearance of buying and selling, there will be no more lawyers. But may not one be richer than another? For two reasons he may not. In the first place, riches give men power to oppress their fellow men and stir up wars. Secondly, riches are impossible to obtain by honest means. A man can never become wealthy by his unaided efforts; and if he is assisted by others, a share in the result of their joint exertions belongs to them. Freedom is to be found only in the unimpeded enjoyment of the land. Property there must be; but all must possess it. All bearers of office must be elected, and none may hold a post for more than one year. Production is to be carried on both by individual and co-operative activity. Each brings what he has produced to the common store, and takes what he needs either for maintenance or for his work. A certain quantum is expected from each, and, if it is not forthcoming, the worker is placed under supervision and if necessary punished. Education, which is universal, includes technical instruction. Work is expected from all under forty, and may be continued after that age at will. Those who have reached the age of sixty superintend the well-being of the entire community. The town and county officials compose the county Parliament and Court. Members of the national Parliament must be over forty, unless specially distinguished, and are chosen by all over twenty. The chief duty of the clergy is to provide instruction on the weekly day of rest, consisting of a relation of the chief events which have happened during the week, readings from the laws of the land, and lectures on subjects of general interest. Marriage is a civil rite, and may be terminated for sufficient reasons by a declaration of the parties before an official and witnesses. Buying and selling are punished with death; and to declare that land is the property of any individual subjects the speaker to branding.

Of Winstanley there is little more to relate. Soon after completing the presentation of his thought, he seems to have joined the Quakers. His latest work, *The Saints' Paradise*, appearing in 1658, combines his old spaciousness of thought with a quietism that is largely new. 'The heart that thinks it cannot live without money, lands, the help of man and creatures, is tempted of the devil; the pure spirit or holy law within tells the heart it must be stript of all these and trust to Providence for subsistence.' Alone of his English contemporaries, he pronounced the well-being of the masses the criterion not only of political institutions, but of social and economic conditions. Convinced that their rights were not secured in the actual state of society, he proceeded to develop a complete scheme of communism. Human nature, he believed, was capable of transformation if certain changes were effected, and if the study of natural science superseded 'fantastic speculations'. But with all his crudities Winstanley can claim to have seen that certain ideas nominally accepted by the conscience of mankind involved far-reaching social and economic transformations, and to have proclaimed that until society was organized on a moral basis no political changes could bear their expected fruit.

CHAPTER VII

THE SECTS

THE opposition to the first two Stuarts arose even more from religious than from political causes; and the sects, both old and new, played a prominent part in the discussion of political principles which filled the years of conflict.

I

As the successful resistance of Scotland to the attack on its religious life led to the summoning of Parliament in 1640, so the assistance of the Scots in 1643 was purchased by the Solemn League and Covenant and the temporary domination of Presbyterian ideas. While most of the English Presbyterians under Elizabeth and James were conformists, their Scottish brethren, who possessed their own Church, were of a much more aggressive type. The sovereignty of the people and the right of deposition, lamented Heylin, their Anglican historian, were principles which no true Scot would dare to question unless he would be thought to betray his country. Even Drummond, the gentle singer of Hawthornden, declared that every prince should study Buchanan and Mariana for his own and the public good. Anglican royalists reserved their special hatred for Presbyterians, whom they classed with Jesuits in their unsleeping hostility to the royal power. The Reformation had overthrown the claim of Rome to dominate secular governments; but the same demand reappeared in the bosom of Protestantism. The State was the servant of the Church and must carry out its behests. The duty of the subject was to obey the Church, and only to obey the magistrate in so far as he executed its commands.

It is in the works of Rutherford that we find the fullest exposition of the political ideas of the northern Presbyterians. 'Every one had in his hand Rutherford's new book, *Lex Rex*', records a contemporary Anglican, 'stuffed with questions that in time of peace would have been judged damnable treason, but were now so idolized that whereas in the beginning Buchanan was looked on as an oracle, he was now slighted as not anti-monarchical enough.' All jurisdiction, he declared, was artificial, its form determined by expediency. If monarchy were chosen, the people should measure out by ounce weights so much royal power and no more, on condition they might resume it if the conditions were violated. In becoming a party to the contract, the king remained strictly the servant of the people. To choose a king was to make a king. Blood constituted no claim, for the origin of monarchy was elective. In like manner Parliament could no more resist the people than could the king. Its power was purely fiduciary, and the people could annul its acts. That the people, however, as a collective entity, should have their way was not to suggest that the component parts might act as they liked.

The most celebrated of English Presbyterians when the struggle opened was Prynne. Imprisoned in 1632 for attacking the Queen in his onslaught on stage plays, he had lost his ears by order of the High Commission, and vowed vengeance on Laud, whom he was one day to hound to his death. His great constitutional treatise, *The Sovereign Power of Parliaments*, printed by order of the Commons in 1643, exercised, we are told by Baxter, immense influence on minds that were wavering. He commences by declaring that, dangerous as the paradox might seem, Parliament was above the King and could enforce his assent to Bills necessary to the common weal. For since Parliament could annul a King's proclamation, it was obviously superior to him. Most justly, by the Law both of Nature and of Nations, might measures directed to their destruction be resisted by the people and the agents be imprisoned; for the King was but the kingdom's public servant. In such cases war was neither treason nor rebellion; for when the nobility joined with the Commons in defence of their ancient liberties, they could not be called rebels. This attitude, however, implied no distaste for monarchy, for the author had always been and would always remain an honourer and defender of kings and kingship. To prove that evil rulers alone suffered from the application of his theory, Prynne reminded his readers of Wenceslas, Mary Stuart, and Philip II. The book was a sustained attempt to throw the mantle of legality over the cause of Parliament by the citation of precedents. But the old judicial supremacy was once more made a basis for the new claim to legislative supremacy, and in demanding the control of the Army and the Great Seal he went beyond the sanction of tradition. In one important respect he differed from nearly all his fellow Presbyterians. An Erastian, like most lawyers, he opposed the establishment even of his own Church and upheld the supremacy of the State.

On the overthrow of Presbyterian predominance by the Army, Prynne's implicit conservatism came to the surface. The Presbyterian majority in Parliament continued to negotiate with Charles even after the renewal of war in 1648. Though he had written hundreds of pages to prove that the deposition of one king and the election of another were authorized by reason and precedent, he now denied that the King could be deposed or his son excluded from the succession. 'No ordinance you can make', he told the dominant party, 'will be any legal bar against his return.' He also strove to procure the acceptance of the royal terms. The House of Lords was passionately defended, not on the ground of its utility, but because it would be 'the extremity of injustice to deny them their ancient hereditary right'. On the abolition of the Monarchy and the House of Lords he turned his weapons against the Oligarchy and the Protectorate. Throughout the unending series of books and pamphlets the law of England is the measure of all things. Charles was the legal heir, and that was now enough for Prynne. 'He asserts the King's right so boldly', wrote a royalist agent, 'that he may be called the Cato of his age.' Of all the sects the Presbyterians were politically the most conservative; and Prynne, who never travelled an inch beyond the ideal of limited monarchy, lived to welcome the Restoration and to sit in the Parliaments of Charles II.

A similar conservatism, though cast rather in a theological than a legal mould, is to be found in the writings of Baxter, the greatest of English Presbyterians. Unlike most clergymen of the State Church, he espoused the Parliamentary cause, and became a military chaplain after Naseby. 'What rare and mighty works have we seen in England for four or five years!' he wrote in *The Saints' Rest* in 1650. 'What a destruction of the enemy! What miracles have taken place, and in what an unhoped-for way!' The later incidents of the struggle, however, had been profoundly distasteful to him. He was never a strong party man. In his Autobiography, written long after, he pronounces both sides to blame; 'but, whoever was faulty, the people's liberties and safety should not be forfeited'. He opposed the extirpation of episcopacy, though he had lost faith in it, and sharply attacked the regicides. Though he did not resist the oligarchy, he sympathized with those who did. Again, when he met the Protector after the only sermon which he preached before him, he told him that he took their ancient monarchy to be a blessing in the land, and asked how England had forfeited it. 'I did openly declare Cromwell and his associates', he wrote in his Autobiography, 'guilty of treason and rebellion.' On the other hand, though it was unlawful to swear allegiance to any governor save the King, it was not unlawful to submit; and he was convinced that in the main it was Oliver's desire to do good. He welcomed the Restoration, became a chaplain to Charles II, and refused a bishopric; but he was driven from the Church by the Act of Uniformity, and lived to be insulted by Jeffreys and to rejoice in the expulsion of James II.

Baxter's political theory was expounded in the *Holy Commonwealth*. The emphatic declaration in the Preface, 'I like not the democratic forms', is an epitome of the treatise. The people's consent is not always necessary to the constitution of the government. The sovereign, he adds in words that reveal a reader of Hobbes, is above all the positive laws of the Commonwealth; for he that is highest hath no higher to obey, and laws are merely expressions of the lawgiver's will. Democratic government is the worst of all forms. Governors must be good as well as wise; but as there are few such men, the good will soon be succeeded by the bad. The unfitness of the mass for responsible posts is proved by a glance round a court. 'I have thought of the excellency of democracy when I have sat and heard a learned judge opening a hard case to a jury, and they have stood by all the while as if he had been talking Greek or Hebrew, and brought in their verdict as it first came to their tongue-ends, before they understood the case any more than the man in the moon, unless there were a crafty fellow among them, and then he rules the rest.' It would often do as well, he adds, to throw dice. He speaks bitterly of the 'ignorant and ungodly rabble', of 'men fetched from the dung-cart to make our laws'. Though government must not be absolute, the effective check is to be sought in the influence of the moral law. Only a very bungling government would molest such a peaceable subject. The fanaticism of reaction is forcibly suggested in the fact that the *Holy Commonwealth* was burned at Oxford in 1683, in company with the writings of Milton and other men whose political doctrines were anathema to him.

After the final defeat of the King, the Presbyterians set themselves to undo the work they had done, and offered to re-establish the royal authority in return for a concession of Presbyterianism for three years. No one believed that their sentiments had really changed, and Charles himself declared them enemies of monarchy. Bishop Bramhall bitterly remarked that if the King would not grant them Presbyterianism they were for the people, and when the people resisted their will they were for the King. Royalists used to say that the Presbyterians brought the King to the block, and the Independents cut off his head. Henry More denounced their Church as a 'democratical Papacy'.

H

To those who did not realize that their politics were dominated by their ecclesiastical ambitions, they naturally appeared 'a crafty and perfidious generation'. Compared with the triumph of the Presbyterian system they cared little for the defence of the constitution or the conquest of new liberties. That it was alien to the English spirit was sorrowfully admitted by its most ardent champions. Parliament was Erastian, the Army Independent, the people indifferent or hostile. Rutherford despaired of 'a reformation', and Baxter, at the end of his life, lamented that 'Presbytery was but a stranger here'. It was adopted under pressure in 1643, and English Puritanism was never genuinely Presbyterian.

The Scottish Presbyterians remained far less royalist than their English brothers. How little they respected monarchy was shown when they had Charles II in their power after the execution of the King. On being compelled to mourn publicly for his own sins and those of his father and grandfather, he remarked in a caustic aside, 'I think I ought to repent too that ever I was born'. At his coronation he was compelled to listen to a sermon of interminable length on the limitation of kingly power. The defeat of Dunbar was relieved of part of its sting by the thought that he was at any rate free from his Presbyterian fetters. When he was restored, mainly by Presbyterians, ten years later, he was strong enough to command their support without accepting their conditions.

II

While the Presbyterians with few exceptions favoured limited monarchy, the Independents formed the main army of republicanism. Their ecclesiastical system predisposed them to democratic views of polity. Men who chose their pastors might also wish to choose their magistrates. Their founder, Robert Brown, taught that any company of Christians formed a Church; and though he set forth the duty to 'esteem, honour and serve the magistrates' in civil matters, it was on the assumption that they were chosen by the people. The implications of the teaching were at once perceived, and several people suffered death for possessing his writings. Thus the thought of the Brownists, as the early Independents were called, was saturated with democratic feeling. Their second founder, Barrow, emphasized the desirability of intercourse and co-operation between different congregations. For a generation the Congregationalists made little progress; but about the middle of the 'thirties their numbers began to grow rapidly. The establishment of Puritan colonies in New England led to the development of the democratic ideas implicit in Independency. Anglican divines lamented that their countrymen fled out of England as out of Babylon. The Fundamental Orders of Connecticut, drawn up for the malcontents who left theocratic Massachusetts under the lead of Hooker, included the sovereignty of the general assembly of citizens and the annual election of officers. No property qualification was demanded, and, except in the case of the Governor, no religious test was imposed. It is significant that the first written constitution of modern democracy was the offspring of the Independents.

During the sessions of the Westminster Assembly the five Independent members attracted attention and aroused hostility by their vigorous defence of toleration. Some members, declared Baillie, denied the lawfulness of any magistrate, and indeed were no better than antinomians. In response to these attacks their leader came forward. John Goodwin, while an Anglican clergyman, had been brought under the notice of Laud for ecclesiastical and doctrinal eccentricities, and his scruples had led him to throw up the appointments his learning had won for him at Cambridge. On the outbreak of war he published a pamphlet on its lawfulness and necessity. The people, he claimed, were not opposing the King, but defending his royal person, honour and estate, endangered by his accursed retinue. To this they were urged by the manifest law of God and the light of nature. It was the duty as well as the right of subjects to examine the commands of their superiors. If the clergy had preached this doctrine instead of the contrary, kings would have a better record in history. 'But as for offering violence to the person of the King and trying to take away his life, I never travelled that way with any desires or thought. It is a just prerogative of the person of kings in what case soever to be secure from the violence of men, and their lives to be as corn, meet to be reaped and gathered only by the hand of God.' Events, however, moved rapidly, and Goodwin moved with them. During the King's trial he issued his *Might and Right well met*. Revolutionary principles are now stated as axioms. 'It is lawful for any man even by violence to wrest a sword out of the hand of a madman, though it be never so legally his.' It was absurd to protest that there was no mandate from the people for an act of sovereign necessity. 'The army conforms to a law of far greater authority than any one, yea, than all the laws of the land put together, the law of nature,

of necessity, and of love to their country, which, being
the law of God, hath a jurisdiction over all human
constitutions. Yea, many of the very laws of God
themselves think it no disparagement to give place to
their elder sister, the law of necessity.' To set the laws
of God and Nature above those of man was the
practice of many democratic controversialists; but to
subject the laws of God to the 'law of necessity' was a
novelty even in that age of speculative audacities.

The more radical element noticeable in Goodwin's
later utterances had been introduced above all by Hugh
Peters, described by the Presbyterian Edwards as
'Vicar-General of the Independents of Old and New
England'. After an early training in Holland and
America he returned to become a chaplain in the
Parliamentary army. His vigorous personality raised
him to a position of exceptional influence, and it was
said that if Peter kept the keys of Heaven, Peters kept
those of the consciences of the Grandees (the chief
officers), opening and shutting them at pleasure. His
earliest pamphlets were not extravagant; but he seems
to have been of a rough and almost brutal nature. If we
may believe Sir Philip Warwick, he worried Laud all
the way from his prison to the scaffold, and when the
King's head fell he repeated the *Nunc Dimittis* in fervent tones. If Lilburne is to be trusted, Peters declared
that Law was the sword and what it gave.

III

Their connexion with the Peasant Revolt of 1525
and the tragi-comedy of Munster was as naturally
asserted by the foes of the Baptists as it was denied
by themselves. The source from which the English

Baptists derived was in fact widely different. Early in the seventeenth century Smyth and Helwisse seceded from the Independent refugees in Amsterdam and adopted the opinions of Menno, who, in addition to antipaedobaptism, had taught that no Christian might swear or carry arms, and that magistrates must be obeyed in all things not contrary to the mind of God. Under this flag he had led off the moderate party after the great conference of Continental Anabaptists in Westphalia in 1536, and since then they had had no relation with the antinomians. When, therefore, Helwisse founded his church in London in 1611 he introduced not the anarchic or communist, but the moderate or Mennonite faith. In common with every other nonconforming body, the Baptists denied the authority of magistrates in matters of religion; but in other ways their political orthodoxy was unimpeachable. In the first declaration, issued in the year 1611, it is declared to be 'a fearful sin to speak evil of them that are in dignity or to despise government'. In their plea for liberty of conscience, issued in 1614, the contention that its concession would not endanger peace or order is repeatedly emphasized. A few years later an address to the King describes them as 'loyal subjects, not for fear only but for conscience sake'. Of similar character are all their manifestoes and petitions before the crisis of 1640.

With the outbreak of war the sect rapidly increased its numbers, and a less quietistic spirit became apparent among certain of its members. 'In all the sects, especially the Anabaptists', wrote Baillie in 1645, 'there is a definite averseness from all obedience to the present magistrates and laws and frequent motions to have the very fundamentals of government new modelled. They do no more dissemble their detestation of monarchy.' Fuller credited them with teaching that a king could not make a good law if he were not perfectly regenerate. These are the tales of the enemy, and the official manifestos of the sect continued to be eminently conservative. But the Baptists had no theoretic preference for monarchy, and they witnessed the execution of the royal victim without emotion. As a sect they never adopted republicanism; but the opinions of some of their more radical members were expressed in a pamphlet entitled *The Golden Rule of Justice Advanced*. The author, Canne, had been a pastor at Amsterdam, and on his return founded Broadmead Chapel. His tract embodied the favourite form of the theory of popular sovereignty. St. Paul merely inculcated obedience lest Christians might imagine they owed none to a heathen magistracy. Assuming agreement that a tyrant may be assassinated, Canne asks why he may not be brought to trial. If the execution of a king after legal process was a novelty, it pointed not to depravity, but to a sense of justice and a love of fair dealing which were new. So far as there was a revolutionary wing to the sect during the Protectorate, it was to be found in the army stationed in Ireland, where a plot was formed to set up an Anabaptist general in 1653. Henry Cromwell complained that they openly denied the position of his father and reviled those who served him. With this exception their record is clear. Baxter, though no friend, confessed that 'most of them were persons of zest in religion and godly, sober people, and differed from others but in the point of infant baptism'. Again, though Jeremy Taylor selects them as an example of an exception that might have to be made in the 'Liberty of Prophesying', it is because they

held it unlawful to take up arms, and other tenets soon
to become characteristic of the most peaceable of men.

IV

Fiery spirits among the Baptists found a more
congenial home with the Fifth Monarchy men. The
abilities and learning of Joseph Mede had given
currency to Millenarian ideas as far back as the
'twenties; but not till the crisis of 1640 did they cease
to be the property of scholars. The very name of the
sect suggests the outlines of a political philosophy.
The fourth monarchy was drawing to a close, and was
to be followed by the reign of the saints. In view of
this great transformation, all political arrangements
now in being became of necessity transitory. So far
all were agreed. But the Millenarians of the English
revolution, like those of the German Reformation,
split over the question of their attitude towards the
existing order. Should they passively await the arrival
of the heavenly kingdom, or should they endeavour to
hasten its advent?

' 'Tis certain', wrote Thurloe to Henry Cromwell in
1655, 'that the Fifth Monarchy men, some of them I
mean, have designs of putting us into blood.' Of the
two wings thus indicated the more moderate may be
traced in the camp after Naseby. Harrison, Overton,
and other officers embraced the Millenarian faith, and
Fleetwood was suspected of something more than
sympathy. After the King's death a pamphleteer
declared that the form but not the power of monarchy
had disappeared, and that Parliament was no less
tyrannical; another that nobles and mighty men were
about to become subject to the saints, and that it was

lawful to combat Christ's enemies with the sword. The chief penman of the party, John Rogers, had been successively an Anglican and a Presbyterian. 'Sagrir, or Domesday drawing nigh', professed to expose the ungodly laws of the fourth monarchy and to announce the approach of the fifth. The origin of all good laws was in the people; but successive conquests had robbed them of their rights. The two plagues of the nation, the priest and the lawyer, must be removed ere the Church of Christ could be reformed. The fourth monarchy was breaking up apace, and would suddenly 'tumble and kick its heels in the air'. By 1666 the fifth would be visible, and by the end of the century it would have prevailed. Men, therefore, should buy no more lands nor estates, seeing it would make such mad work in the world. A further tract urged the saints to join no religious organization. No compulsion should be exerted on action or thought, and magistrates were superfluous.

Harrison's share in the expulsion of the Rump, together with Rogers' hopeful appeal to the Protector and Oliver's gentle references to the sect, prove that the party did not oppose the new régime. They fixed their hopes on the Barebones Parliament, which was largely composed of their own adherents. Nor did the Assembly disappoint their expectations. It attacked the clergy, demanded the abolition of Chancery, and declared nobility contrary to the Law of Nature. 'Their prate', declared a royalist historian, 'was to make way for Christ's Monarchy on earth.' But on the dissolution of the Parliament the sect broke with the Protector. Harrison began to plot and was arrested. Rogers denounced Oliver as Anti-Christ, the Man of Sin, the Great Dragon. Many believed that Christ would appear in 1656, because the ages of the patriarchs in Genesis added together reached that number. The leader of the party of action was Feake. 'Lord', he prayed, 'Thou hast suffered us to cut off the head which reigned over us, and Thou hast suffered the tail to set itself up and rule over us in the head's place.' He was arrested; but when the government spy again visited the meeting at Blackfriars he found the place crowded —'the humours boiling, and as much scum came off as ever'. Feake declared at his trial that God would destroy not only unlawful but lawful government, not only the abuse but the use of it. It was debated at a meeting when was the time for destroying Babylon, who should do it and how it should be done. The meeting resolved that the saints must do it, 'the time to be now and the means the sword'. The resolution was quickly put into practice, for in 1657 their first insurrection broke out. 'The number and quality of the persons engaged', reported Thurloe to the Council, 'were truly very inconsiderable and indeed despicable. Though they speak great words of the reign of the saints and seem to invite none but the holy seed, yet the baits they lay to catch men are the taking away customs, excise, taxes, tithes.' Public opinion, none the less, was thoroughly alarmed. 'These incendiaries', wrote Henry Cromwell, 'are very dangerous and of an inveterate temper.' A cipher list of names marked for destruction was discovered. Many taught that all the ungodly must be killed and that the wicked had no property in their estate. Ere long the saints would take over the possessions of the wicked and the reign of Christ would begin. Such men naturally did not trouble themselves with the trivialities of constitution-making.

Alone of the sects the Fifth Monarchy men refused to accept the Restoration without a struggle. Harrison died with the conviction that he would shortly return at the right hand of Christ to judge his judges. In this spirit, some nine months after the return of the King, a small body of them broke into St. Paul's, asking the first person they met for whom he was. 'For King Charles', was the reply, whereon he was shot by the rebels with the words, 'We are for King Jesus'. But Venner's revolt was quickly suppressed, and the Millenarianism of action disappears from English history. The Fifth Monarchy men were the only genuinely explosive sect during the years of confusion; and their history most clearly reveals the inextricable confusion of religion and politics.

v

By far the most important of the sects which sprang up during the years of revolution were the Quakers, whom the critics were at first puzzled how to classify. Some declared them an offshoot of Anabaptism. Baxter, after describing the Ranters and naïvely adding that they were so few that he had never seen one, declares that the Quakers were the same sect under another name. Another critic contented himself with declaring that the Ranters and Quakers were 'unclean beasts, much of the same puddle'. In reality the new movement most resembled the Mennonite Church, whence the Baptists had already sprung. The General Baptists, indeed, went over almost in a body to the Friends, and in the rare instances where Quakers deserted their communion they rejoined the Baptists. Yet the spirit was new, for the Quakers were pledged to no definite opinions nor observances. The wayfaring man, as described by Fox, had visited in turn the Papists, the Common-Prayer men, the Presbyterians, the Independents, the Baptists, but by none had he been told that the only religion was that of spirit and of truth. So novel was the attitude that the Anglican Thorndike declared that the Quakers were not to be reckoned as Christians at all.

It is not surprising that the movement appealed to the lower classes as no other sect had done. Against no other body was the accusation brought that it was 'made up of the dregs of the common people'. A friendly critic pointed out that by reclaiming 'such as neither magistrate nor minister ever speak to' it did the law yeoman service. Distinctions of sex no less than class were obliterated. So numerous were the female members that it was at first rumoured that the sect was confined to them. 'Are women priests?' asked Fox, and answered, 'Yes, women are priests'. Another unnatural distinction was equally inadmissible. Clarkson used to say that Fox was the first Englishman publicly to denounce slavery, and more than one slave-owner received a letter warning him that God was no respecter of persons. Combining the priesthood of every believer with the supremacy of the Inner Light, the movement could only be democratic; but the character of the founder went far to keep its individualism from degenerating into anarchy. Fox, though a thorough mystic, steadily opposed every sort of antinomianism. 'Any such as cry, "Away with your laws, we will have none of your laws", are sons of Belial.' He warmly repudiated the charge of political disaffection. 'You speak of the Quakers spreading seditious books and papers. I answer, we have no

seditious books or papers. Our books are against
sedition and seditious men and seditious ways.' As
presented by Fox and his immediate followers, there
was nothing in Quakerism to interfere with the per-
formance of the ordinary duties of citizenship. Cromwell was annoyed at the disturbance of ministers, and
issued a Proclamation threatening penalties. Moreover, he disliked the refusal to pay the customary marks
of respect to magistrates and others in authority. But
he allowed Fox to remain covered in his presence, and
he was well aware that he had no more sterling subjects
than the men who dedicated their lives to a war on
social and moral abuses. On one occasion only did Fox
meddle directly with politics. When the report spread
abroad that Oliver would become King, 'I warned him
against the issue of divers dangers, which, if he did not
avoid, would bring shame and misery on himself and
his posterity. He seemed to take it well and thanked
me.' The Protector knew that his friend and critic
opposed the change solely from fear that it might
inflict spiritual injury by turning him to thoughts of
personal glory.

It was, however, with the few turbulent spirits of
the sect that the age connected the Quaker movement.
In the teaching and conduct of the founder himself
there was a vein of exaltation bordering on fanaticism.
He commenced his apostolate by interrupting a
sermon. Lichfield was denounced as 'a bloody city',
where martyrdoms had taken place under Diocletian.
But though such extravagances were soon outgrown,
the inrush of Baptists and Millenarians gave the movement a bad name for a few years. In 1654 news reached
the government of 'various tumultuous meetings by
persons under the name of Quakers' in the Midlands.

Though they were never seen with a weapon in their hands, some were found carrying pistols under their cloaks. A crazed Quaker took up his position with a sword at the doors of Parliament, declaring that he was inspired to kill every man that sat in the House. In 1655 Henry Cromwell was convinced that he had to deal with a serious problem. 'Our most considerable enemies', he wrote from Ireland to Thurloe, 'are the Quakers. Some of our soldiers have been perverted by them, and I think their principles and practices not very consistent with civil government, much less with the discipline of an army. Some think they have no design; but I am not of that opinion. Their counterfeited simplicity renders them the more dangerous.' Large numbers also crossed the Scottish border, and Baillie believed they were possessed with a devil. 'They furiously cry down magistracy and ministry, and their irrational passions and bodily convulsions are very great.' The people were called to arms on the score that 'the Quakers were up'. A childish panic sometimes prevailed. 'When a great storm arose', relates Anthony Wood, 'some thought the Anabaptists and Quakers were coming to cut their throats.' In some cases Quakers outraged opinion by appearing in public places without clothes. Their antinomianism was most clearly exhibited in the American colonies. 'When they came over in 1657', writes Cotton Mather, 'they induced many to oppose good order, sacred and civil. They manifested an intolerable contempt of authority.' These violent spirits were, however, soon followed by men of a quieter type, and the harmlessness of the sect was gradually recognized.

No member of the left wing of the movement created such consternation as James Naylor, a man of deep spirituality, who had fought in the Parliamentary army and felt a call on hearing Fox. His success as an itinerant preacher turned his head. While residing near Bristol an hallucination seized certain women of his following. Naylor was hailed as the Messiah, the King of Israel, and accepted the title. Though not actually mad, his mind was temporarily unhinged. Recantation failed to mollify his judges, and he was savagely punished. The tragi comedy of Bristol and the collapse of its hero gave a sensible check to the revolutionary current of Quakerism. A few petitioned against the recall of the King and some even sold their land to raise money for the defence of the Commonwealth; but they quickly accepted the inevitable. When the Quaker philosophy took systematic shape with the publication of Barclay's *Apology* in 1676, the tenet of political submissiveness assumed the place from which it has never been removed.

CHAPTER VIII

THE RESTORATION

I

'SUCH a restoration', wrote the gentle royalist Evelyn in his diary on the day of the King's entry into London, 'has never been seen since the return of the Jews.' 'We submit and oblige ourselves and our posterities to your Majesty for ever', declared the Commons. The Convention Parliament quickly made way for the Cavalier Parliament, and an Anglican Chamber was substituted for one largely Presbyterian. The tide of reaction mounted rapidly. Harrington was sent to the Tower, and Milton's works were burned by the common hangman. The Press was effectually gagged by Roger L'Estrange, and Butler's *Hudibras*, with its racy wit and vitriolic satire, was welcomed with transports of delight. It was an axiom in Royalist circles that every Dissenter was a rebel, and only awaited the opportunity to restore the Commonwealth.

Charles was half French by blood and more than half French by temperament and in his view of the royal power. But though he rejected the doctrine of limited monarchy, he found it convenient to be able to transfer the odium of unpopular measures to a minister, and he was resolved 'never to go on his travels again'. His indifference to religion inclined him to toleration, though he recognized the political value of an established Church. In an age of passionate royalism he stood for moderation. He was alive to new ideas, and Clarendon declared with some bitterness that he had 'so little reverence and esteem for antiquity and so much condemns old orders, forms and institutions that the objection of novelty rather advanced than obstructed any proposition'. Moreover, though the country was unfeignedly delighted to return to settled government, the atmosphere was no longer what it had been before the Civil War. The scene outside Whitehall could not be forgotten. The King was aware of the limitations of his power, and the people were conscious of their strength. Even the Cavalier Parliament took care to retain the purse-strings in their hands. Clarendon, who told his master that Parliament was more or less or nothing as he chose to make it, was to learn that it was strong enough to overthrow a powerful minister. The Anglican Church, like the Bourbons, had learned nothing and forgotten nothing during the years of misfortune; for its views of the prerogative were as extravagant and its hatred of Dissent as vindictive as ever. The Corporation Act required all office-holders in corporations to swear that it was unlawful 'upon any pretence whatever', to take arms against the King. The Act of Uniformity expelled two thousand clergy and permanently dismembered the Church. Venner's insignificant rising in the City served to confirm the prejudice that Dissenters were wedded to sedition. Men's nerves were unhinged by the convulsions that they had witnessed, and the worst excesses of the Restoration may be charitably attributed as much to panic as to intolerance.

As the reign advanced Parliament became divided into the Court and Country parties. It was impossible for decent people to reverence a king who turned Whitehall into Vanity Fair; and the rapidly increasing industrial and commercial classes, largely Noncon-

I

formist in conviction, wholly lacked the devotional
feeling for royalty which animated Anglican circles.
The Popish Plot and the introduction of the Exclusion
Bill wrought English politics to fever heat. The
debates on the exclusion of a Catholic heir revived the
discussion of the location of sovereignty, and the rapid
rise of an organised Whig and Tory party gave an
impetus to literary controversy. As the Tories possessed no publicist above the calibre of L'Estrange, a
vigorous though scurrilous pamphleteer, they fell back
on Filmer, who had died in 1653. Though he suffered
imprisonment during the Civil Wars, he played an
insignificant part in the great drama, and his writings
were scarcely noticed in the great flood of pamphlets
which issued from every quarter. His most important
work, the *Patriarcha, or the Natural Power of Kings*,
was not published till 1680. The book derives its
fame largely from the fact that it was answered by
Algernon Sidney and Locke; but it is also of importance as the most powerful statement of a theory which
found numerous adherents throughout the century.

'With no small content', wrote Filmer, 'I read Mr.
Hobbes's book, *De Cive*. I consent with him about the
rights of exercising government, but I cannot agree to
his means of acquiring it.' Mankind was not originally
free nor at liberty to choose a government. This
notion had been originated by the Schoolmen, adopted
by certain Protestant divines, and welcomed by the
common people as an acknowledgement of their right
to some share of liberty. There is, however, no trace
of such primitive freedom in the Fathers or Scripture,
in the ancient world or the Law of Nature. The
natural liberty and equality of men was the foundation
of sedition; for if supreme power was originally in the

people, only a democracy would be lawful. When this error had been overthrown, the last stronghold of treason would be destroyed. Of what character, then, was primitive society? The origin of government, replies Filmer, was not a surrender of natural rights, but an enlargement of the microcosm of the family. The State is the extension of the family, the King being the father, the people his children. Since Adam and the Patriarchs exercised legal rights over their children, the natural condition of mankind was not equality, but patriarchal rule. Monarchy was at once a divine institution and in accordance with the teachings of nature. A contract between king and people was no more necessary than between a father and his children. 'The father governs by his own will, not by the laws and wills of his sons and servants.' Paternal authority, the only inalienable natural right, was preserved in every monarchical State. This authority, moreover, is as absolute as if it had been conferred by the simultaneous surrender of private rights. 'As kingly power is the law of God, so it hath no inferior power to limit it.' The King had often been described as the father of his people; but it was Filmer's task to translate the metaphor into an argument for absolutism. Laws made in Parliament may be mitigated or suspended for reasons known only to him. His coronation oath only binds him to observe good laws, of which he is the judge. A subject must obey his commands against the law, and even, in some cases, against divine laws. Parliament is purely consultative, and of the two Houses the Commons are the least. The Lords advise, the Commons consent and the King ordains. The alternative to monarchy is anarchy or military despotism. Moreover, it alone can preserve religion as well as order—witness Holland and Venice, the former of which has all religions and the latter none. If there is no heir, a new ruler must be chosen by the heads of the great families; and 'he that is so elected claims not his power as a donative from the people but as being substituted by God'.

Even if Filmer's theory of the origin of government were correct, it does not follow that the unfettered power of the father in early society involves autocracy in a later and widely different age. He admits that Adam's heir is not to be found, and he makes no attempt to prove that the Stuart kings are descended from the Patriarchs. There have been so many usurpations and elections that the argument from descent is abandoned as untenable. He is thus forced into a position perilously near that of Hobbes. 'There is a natural right of a supreme father over every multitude, although many at first do most unjustly obtain the exercise of it.' Thus divine appointment is claimed for the descendants of usurpers. But while the patriarchal hypothesis had no real relevance to the controversy between the Stuarts and their subjects, the conception itself was not less but more historical than the rival dogma of the social contract. Kinship has been the base of many communities, and chieftain-ship has often become hereditary in a single family. Again, in teaching that monarchy developed out of human relationships, it suggests that the State is an organism capable of development, not a mechanical contrivance. These deeper aspects of the theory, however, were little discussed, and Locke roughly declared that so much glib nonsense was never put together in well-sounding English.

Before Locke wrote his essays on Civil Government,

Algernon Sidney had taken up the challenge thrown down by Filmer. The republican aristocrat was among the most interesting personalities of his time, and his tragic end enrolled him among the martyrs of liberty. The son of the second Earl of Leicester and of a Percy, the brother of Waller's Sacharissa, Sidney grew up among refined and gracious influences. Though his father was a royalist, Algernon sided with Parliament and fought gallantly at Marston Moor. 'From my youth up', he declared on the day of his death, 'I endeavoured to uphold the common rights of mankind, the laws of this land and the true Protestant religion against corrupt principles, arbitrary power and popery.' But though a wholehearted supporter of the Parliamentary cause he opposed the execution of the King. Appointed a commissioner for his trial, he declared that the King could be tried by no court, and after his ineffectual protest left the room. His preference, it seems, was for deposition. Elected to the Council of State shortly before the expulsion of the Rump, he witnessed that scene of violence and declared the Protector a tyrant. When the Long Parliament was restored in 1659 he returned to his seat and was admitted to the executive.

Sidney was willing to accept and even to serve a king whom Parliament had recognized. But he had no desire to live in danger of arrest, and he refused to curry favour by expressions of penitence. Being absent in Denmark on an embassy when the Restoration took place, he wandered about Europe for many years. Embittered by plots against his life, he invited Louis XIV to supply him with money to raise a revolt in England; but the French monarch offered a sum too small to be of use. In 1677 he finally obtained leave to return for private business. His intention to stay only three months was abandoned, for the situation was becoming critical and he had made no promise to abstain from public activity. Though his attempts to enter Parliament failed, he was none the less acclaimed as a leader by surviving republicans and the more advanced Whigs. He accepted money from the French Ambassador, whose master he tried to persuade that a republic would be less hostile to France than the Prince of Orange. In his passion for English liberty he shut his eyes to the danger of increasing the power of Louis in Europe. He discussed insurrection with Russell and Essex, and was arrested after the Rye House Plot. Charged with treason, and tried by Jeffreys, he was beheaded on Tower Hill in 1683.

Among the grounds of treason alleged against him was that he had written a book maintaining the subjection of the King to Parliament and the lawfulness of deposing rulers. The prisoner replied that it was merely an answer to the speculations of Filmer, and that he had no intention of publishing it. The *Discourses concerning Government* were printed in 1698, and were eagerly studied in the Old and the New World, in the original and in French translations, throughout the eighteenth century. This famous work suffers from the fact that it is in part a polemical reply as well as a philosophic treatise, and the advance of his thought is interrupted by a multitude of petty skirmishes; but its general trend is clear enough. The fundamental thesis is that all lawful government rests on consent. Examples are drawn from the history of the Jews, Greeks, Romans and modern European States to prove that national happiness is only to be found where rights and liberties are guaranteed. God has

implanted the principle of liberty in our breasts—not
the liberty to do what is pleasant to man and hateful to
God, but exemption from the authority of laws to
which the people have never assented. The rights of
a people proceed from nature, and men are justified in
using the reason God has given them to examine the
laws and governments under which they live. Princes
are men, not gods. Are we to suffer an evil ruler till
all goodness and virtue are overthrown? Why is it
worse to say that a king should be subject to the
censures of the people than that the people should be
subject to the will of a king? Do the people make the
king or the king the people? The common sense of
mankind has long ago answered these questions.
Throughout the ages tyrants have been held up to
scorn, and the deliverers have been exalted. Tyranny
would collapse if it were universally recognized that
nations have a right to make their own laws and that
the rulers they choose must render an account of their
stewardship.

If it is objected that this course of reasoning makes
God the author of democracy, Sidney rejoins that
God has given power to no man or group of men.
There is no trace of the divine right of kings among the
Jews. He quotes with approval the oath of allegiance
in Aragon. 'We, who are as good as you, make you
our King, on condition that you maintain our liberties
and privileges.' In early England kings were made by
the voice of the people. No species of government is
divine, and man freely chooses what seems best to
him. So far from an absolute, hereditary monarchy
being the best of forms, a system in which power
descends without regard to age, virtue or ability is
incapable of rational defence. No man is good enough

to be trusted with absolute power. True stability only exists where kings are controlled by laws and their defects are supplied by Parliaments. The best governments are a mixture of monarchy, aristocracy and democracy. Pure monarchy is too despotic, pure aristocracy too exclusive, pure democracy only fit for small towns.

Though the treatise is mainly academic, the author's views of the political situation peep out at intervals. Would Hyde and Clifford, Arlington and Danby, he asks, have climbed to the chief places if a free Parliament had had their disposal? Had the duchesses of Cleveland and Portsmouth, and others of the same trade, attained their riches and honours by services to the State? These abuses were the more deplorable since our constitution was in its essence popular. The absolute power of our kings was usurped, for Parliaments were as old as the nation. 'There was never a time when councils or assemblies did not make or unmake laws as they pleased.' The king was above his subjects, but the law was above the king. The Israelites who obeyed Jeroboam, Ahab and other wicked rulers were punished for their disobedience to God. That king is lawful whom the people acknowledge. If a king refuses to summon Parliament, the people must do it; for without Parliament we are a rudderless vessel. But Parliament, too, should be bound by the law it makes, instead of being debased to the private ends of a few men. The ministers of Charles II, he declares bitterly, found a Parliament full of lewd young men, and deliberately corrupted them. Though there was not a word of treason in the book, its pages offered a sustained and powerful argument against the system of personal rule which had been re-established in 1660.

Sidney's political theory is neither highly original nor wholly logical; but his writings glow with conviction and are the product of careful thought. One of the main features of the *Discourses* is their erudition. Burnet declares that he had studied the history of government beyond any man he ever knew; and indeed we hear far more of the historical sanction than of the law of nature. The keynote of his attack on absolutism is the coincidence of the teaching of instinct and experience. So far, however, from being, as Burnet declared, 'stiff to all republican principles and an enemy to everything that looked like monarchy', he fully recognized the need of flexibility. He never forgot that he was an aristocrat, and he insists on the actual inequality of men. 'Such as are base, ignorant, vicious, slothful or cowardly are not equal in natural or acquired virtues to the generous, wise, valiant and industrious, nor equally useful to the societies in which they live; they cannot, therefore, have an equal part in the government of them.' Virtue alone carries a claim to power. Sir William Temple remarked that one passage of the *Discourses* explained the whole. If there was such a thing as divine right, Sidney had written, it was where one man was better qualified to govern others than they were to govern themselves. 'Now I assure you', said Temple, 'he looked on himself as that very man so qualified to govern the rest of mankind.' This malicious thrust need not be taken too seriously. Sidney's idol was liberty, and his historical studies taught him that it might be found under different constitutional guises. He was essentially a moderate, and it is sufficient condemnation of the Restoration system that such a man perished on the scaffold.

Sidney lived and died in steadfast adherence to his principles, and left an abiding impression on those with whom he came in contact. Charles II, a good judge of ability, spoke of him as '*un homme de cœur et d'esprit*', but added that he could not be too far from England, 'where his pernicious sentiments, supported with so great parts and courage, might do much hurt'. Burnet described him as 'a man of most extraordinary courage, a steady man even to obstinacy, sincere but of a rough and boisterous temper, that could not bear contradiction'. He adds that he seemed a Christian, 'but in a particular form of his own. He thought it was to be like a divine philosophy in the mind; but he was against all public worship and everything that looked like a Church.' All that Sidney's own writings reveal is a hatred of Catholicism and of intolerance. Though he does not rank as a political thinker of the first class, like Hobbes, Harrington, and Halifax, he deserved well of his country in keeping alive the flame of liberty in the dark days of the Restoration.

II

The Exclusion crisis brought ecclesiastical as well as lay controversialists into the arena. The most effective of these militant clergy was Samuel Johnson, the chaplain of Lord William Russell, who was launched on a political career by a sermon before the Lord Mayor in 1679 in which, under cover of an attack on Popery, he indirectly supported the Exclusion Bill. When Hickes, the learned Anglican who was soon to become a nonjuror, published a discourse on the sovereign power, Johnson retorted with his most celebrated work, *Julian the Apostate*. It was obvious

to every reader that Catholicism was modern pagan-
ism, and the Duke of York the apostate Emperor.
With such a ruler, he argued, it was ridiculous to talk
of unconditional obedience. He maintained that the
early Christians had neither held nor practised the
doctrine of non-resistance, that they had tried to
prevent Julian's accession, and that they resisted his
attacks on Christianity. Resistance for the safeguard-
ing of religion was as lawful in the seventeenth as in
the fourth century. St. Paul had said nothing about
tyrants, and the law of the land was the best exposition
of the thirteenth chapter of Romans. Men were
naturally free, and could be bound only by their own
act and deed. The spectacle of an Anglican divine
attacking the doctrine for which his Church had stood
for nearly a century aroused intense interest, and the
Julian was eagerly read and provoked many replies. The
book was publicly burned, and he was imprisoned for
a libel on the Duke of York. He was detested by the
Royalists, and Dryden bespattered him with abuse in
Absalom and Achitophel—

> Let Hebron [Scotland] nay let Hell, produce a man
> So made for mischief as Ben Jochanan.

When Burnet tried to persuade Lord William Russell
to save his life by disowning the principle of resistance,
Johnson encouraged his old master to stand firm.

On the accession of James to the throne, Johnson
succeeded in smuggling out of his prison a tract which
rivalled *Julian* in importance and popularity. His
Address to the Protestants in King James's Army
adjured officers and soldiers not to aid the enslavement
of the country or to ruin the national religion. The
pamphlet was remarkable for its forcible style, and

the Government paid it the compliment of savagely punishing its author. When a thousand copies had been distributed the rest were seized. But though the author was whipped from Newgate to Tyburn, his spirit was unbroken. He used the freedom which he regained by the Declaration of Indulgence in 1687 to renew the war against Catholics and to urge the Church to open its doors to Nonconformists. Calamy, indeed, records that he was generally considered to have done more than any other man to prepare the Revolution of 1688. Scouting the refinements of timid Whigs, he boldly declared that William had but one plain title, the gift of the people. Compensation was voted to the Whig confessor by Parliament, who, however, did not receive the promotion which he deemed his due. The man whom Swift called Julian Johnson was a rough controversialist, lacking distinction and refinement; but his vigorous blows helped to checkmate the royal campaign, and he possesses the distinction of being the first Anglican divine to have stood boldly forth against the Catholic King. His work was of peculiar value to his party in an age when royalists invariably appealed to the authority of the Bible. 'I do not know', declares Coleridge, 'where I could put my hand on a book containing so much sense and sound constitutional doctrine as this thin folio of Johnson's works.'

In the fierce strife which called Sidney and Johnson into the field a more imposing figure sprang to the aid of the royal cause. After years devoted to the production of heroic dramas, Dryden returned to his poetry, and produced the rhymed polemics and manifestos which make him the greatest satirist in the language. The Poet Laureate was a notorious weathercock. His first considerable poem was in praise of

Cromwell, his second a fulsome paean to Charles II on his restoration. At the instigation of the Government he had written his tragedy, *Amboyna*, to inflame the nation against the Dutch. When the Popish Plot had scared credulous Protestants out of their senses, he bitterly assailed the Catholic priesthood in *The Spanish Friar*. As the tide began to turn he pilloried Monmouth and his supporters in *The Duke of Guise*.

In the autumn of 1681, when Shaftesbury was about to be tried for treason, appeared *Absalom and Achitophel*. Though the staunch Whiggism of the City threw out the bill against the Whig leader, thus defeating the immediate object of the poem, it did more than any other work of the time to turn the fortunes of the struggle in favour of the King. Dr. Johnson's father, an old bookseller, told his son that he remembered no such success except the narrative of the trial of Dr. Sacheverell thirty years later. The parallel of Absalom and Monmouth was so obvious that it had been adopted before Dryden wrote. With the instinct of the experienced dramatist, he substituted for abstract denunciation of sedition and treason a concrete presentation of the leaders of the opposing armies under the transparent disguise of Jewish history. The matchless vigour of the verse electrified alike friend and foe. Such concentrated invective, such vivacity, such power of stinging satire was hitherto unknown. Though not a politician Dryden was by far the most effective Tory controversialist of his age.

The portrait of Monmouth is drawn more in sorrow than in anger. Dryden had received kindnesses from the Duke and the Duchess, and he knew the tender feeling of Charles for his son.

> Unblamed of life (ambition set aside),
> Not stained with cruelty nor puffed with pride,
> How happy had he been if Destiny
> Had higher placed his birth or not so high.

The whole blame of his political escapades is attributed to the tempter Shaftesbury. Of all the opponents of the King, 'a monarch after Heaven's own heart', the great Whig leader is described as the worst in lines of concentrated passion which burn after two centuries.

> Of these the false Achitophel was first,
> A name to all succeeding ages curst;
> For close designs and crooked counsels fit,
> Sagacious, bold and turbulent of wit;
> Restless, unfixed in principles and place,
> In power unpleased, impatient of disgrace.
> A daring pilot in extremity,
> Pleased with the danger, when the waves went high,
> He sought the storms.
> In friendship false, implacable in hate,
> Resolved the ruin or to rule the State.

While Shaftesbury is the butt of the poet's most savage attack, minor actors are sketched with no less power and skill. The famous picture of Buckingham, the son of the favourite of Charles I and the playfellow of Charles II, conveys in a few brilliant strokes the great nobleman who coquetted with politics and literature.

> A man so various that he seemed to be
> Not one but all mankind's epitome.
> Stiff in opinions, always in the wrong,
> Was everything by starts and nothing long;
> But in the course of one revolving moon
> Was chymist, fiddler, statesman and buffoon;
> Then all for women, painting, rhyming, drinking,
> Besides ten thousand freaks that died in thinking.

In sharp contrast to Zimri stood Barzilai, the noble Ormond, 'crowned with honour and with years'.

In exile with his godlike prince he mourned,
For him he suffered and with him returned.
The Court he practised, not the courtier's art;
Large was his wealth, but larger was his heart.

Among the smaller figures on the canvas none is drawn with more consummate skill than Slingsby Bethel, the Republican Sheriff of the City—

Shimei, whose youth did early promise bring
Of zeal to God and hatred to his King,
Did wisely from expensive sins refrain
And never broke the Sabbath but for gain;
Nor ever was he known on oath to vent,
Or curse, unless against the Government.
The City, to reward his pious hate
Against his master, chose him magistrate.
If any durst his factious friends accuse,
He packed a jury of dissenting Jews;
Whose fellow-feeling in the godly cause
Would free the suffering saint from human laws.
For laws are only made to punish those
Who serve the King, and to protect his foes.
His business was by writing to persuade
That Kings were useless and a clog to trade.

Shaftesbury's life was saved by the Grand Jury in the City, and the failure of the prosecution was commemorated by the striking of a medal. Dryden promptly returned to the charge in a shorter poem, *The Medal, or a Satire against Sedition.* The invective against Shaftesbury is as violent as ever—

So like a man, so golden to the sight,
So base within, so counterfeit and light.
He preaches to the crowd that power is lent,
But not conveyed to kingly government;
Maintains the multitude can never err,
And sets the people in the papal chair.

Among the many Whig champions who took up the gauntlet was Shadwell, a rival dramatist, on whom Dryden savagely turned in a third satire, *MacFlecknoe.*

Flecknoe was an eccentric minor poet recently deceased, who—

> In prose and verse was owned, without dispute,
> Through all the realms of nonsense absolute,

and who is made to hail Shadwell as his heir and 'perfect image'. But in this, and in the second part of *Absalom and Achitophel*, which followed it, there is something disproportionate in the heavy ordnance directed against such small craft.

Dryden's *Religio Laici*, a manifesto both against Catholicism and Dissent, had expressed his Protestant convictions, and his struggle against the Exclusionists was carried on from the Protestant camp. But early in the reign of James II the poet became a Catholic, though there is no need to connect the change with ambition or the hope of gain. He hastened to explain and defend his new attitude in the last of his great didactic poems, *The Hind and the Panther*, published in 1687. The Roman Church naturally occupies the first place in the poet's affections—

> A milk-white Hind, immortal and unchanged,
> Without unspotted, innocent within,
> She feared no danger, for she knew no sin.

He also speaks with relative friendliness of his old communion—

> The Panther, sure the noblest next to Hind,
> And fairest creature of the spotted kind.
> Oh! could her inborn stains be washed away,
> She were too good to be a beast of prey.

The First Part treats the Dissenters with extreme severity; but as the author became aware of the King's intention to conciliate them by a general Indulgence, he endeavoured to make amends in the Third Part and in the Preface. The poem revealed undiminished vigour and contains many beautiful passages; but it exerted no influence on opinion or policy, and with the Revolution he lost the Laureateship and his pension, paying the penalty of his sensational triumph as a Tory propagandist.

The attempt to exclude James from the succession was a gigantic blunder. The violence of the Whigs played into the hands of the King, who found himself by no virtue of his own in a stronger position at the end of his reign than he had been at any period of its course. The near approach of a second civil war frightened the nation into an outburst of loyalty, and language was employed which had not been heard since the days of Charles I. The high-water mark of servility was reached in the decrees of Oxford University in 1683, when Convocation condemned twenty-seven propositions, among them that civil authority is derived from the people, that a mutual compact exists between the ruler and his subjects, and that the King might be over-ruled by Lords and Commons. The tenets of Millenarians and Quakers were bracketed with those of Milton and Baxter, Owen and Johnson; and Hobbes, who would have been surprised to find himself in such company, is denounced for teaching that possession confers a right to obedience.

Such academic Byzantinism possessed no great significance while Charles was on the throne; but when he was succeeded by his Catholic brother the exaltation of the royal prerogative wore a more threatening aspect. The danger to English liberties was revealed in a flash by the judgement of the Lord Chief Justice in the collusive action against Sir Edward Hales, whom the King, in defiance of the Test Act, had appointed

K

Governor of Dover Castle. The King, he declared, was an absolute prince; the laws were his and the construction of them belonged to him. The King could not part with any branch of his prerogative, nor could Parliament limit him, even with his consent, in the choice of his servants. 'There is no law whatsoever but may be dispensed with by the supreme lawgiver, as the law of God may be dispensed with by God himself.' The judgement fell like a thunderbolt, and Tories agreed with Whigs that if such principles went unchallenged, the fabric of Protestantism would soon lie in ruins. In face of such a threat to the national faith the paralysing doctrine of non-resistance faded away like a cloud. The consummation of a century's evolution was registered in the resolution of the Convention Parliament that the power of the Crown was derived from an original contract between the King and the people, that the contract had been broken by James II, and that the throne was vacant. The Divinity of Kings, which had entered England with James I, left it for ever in the baggage of his grandson.

CHAPTER IX

HALIFAX

THE most subtle and original thinker of the Restoration era stood aloof from the fierce conflict of Whigs and Tories, and pursued his way undeterred by the shower of missiles which assailed him from every quarter. Though his statesmanship was vindicated by Macaulay, it is only in recent years that the writings of the Prince of Trimmers have won their rightful place among the classics of political literature.

George Savile was connected by blood or marriage with many of the most distinguished men of his century, with Strafford and Sidney, with Shaftesbury and Sunderland. Though his father fought for the King, his early death in 1643, before passions had become embittered, saved his large estates from confiscation; and when the son came of age in 1654 he found himself one of the wealthiest men in the kingdom. In the Cavalier Parliament he joined his uncle Coventry and his friend Buckingham in the attack which culminated in the fall of Clarendon, and his services were rewarded by the title of Viscount Halifax. While giving a general support to the Cabal he welcomed the Test Act, which broke up the hybrid ministry and drove the Duke of York from his office in the Admiralty. Startled by the strength of Protestant feeling, the King abandoned *la grande affaire* of the conversion of England. When Danby succeeded the Cabal Halifax joined Shaftesbury in opposition, and on the fall of the minister in 1679 obtained office for the first time. At this point the most critical period of his life begins. It was the aim of the Whig leader to exclude the Duke of York from the succession on the ground that he was an acknowledged Catholic. Halifax, on the other hand, though he disliked Catholicism as heartily as his uncle, set his face like flint against the project on the ground that it would involve civil war, and that all danger to Protestantism could be avoided by the imposition of restrictions on the monarch. Indeed, according to Burnet, he privately explained to the Whig leaders that his position was the more advanced, since the terms on which he proposed to allow James to succeed virtually amounted to republican government. His advice to the King to dissolve the Parliament of 1679 led the country party to declare him a traitor, and his promotion to an earldom registered his advance in the royal favour. But though he had a weakness for titles, his support of the royal interest was the result of deep conviction. When the Exclusion Bill reached the Lords in 1681 and the country was in a fever of excitement, his prolonged oratorical duel with Shaftesbury secured its rejection by a narrow majority. This supreme service was rewarded by elevation to the rank of Marquis.

In the fierce strife of party which filled the later years of Charles II, Halifax played a moderating part. A Conservative by temperament, his mind was a nicely-balanced instrument, sensitive to the needs and currents of the moment. Urbane and philosophic, he hated violence, cruelty and revenge. He opposed the execution both of Lord Stafford and Algernon Sidney. That he worked with different men and was now in opposition, now in office, led fiery partisans to believe that he was merely a time-server, ever ready to desert a sinking ship or to worship the rising sun. To vindicate his character and his creed he wrote *The Character of a Trimmer* in the last days of 1684. As it was thought unlikely that a licence would be granted, it circulated anonymously in manuscript copies till it appeared in print in 1688. The proximate cause of its composition was a resounding attack on the policy of moderation by Roger L'Estrange in *The Observator*. 'A Trimmer', declared the famous Tory journalist, 'is a man of latitude, as well in politics as divinity; a kind of comprehensive Christian that makes more conscience of indulging a division from the Church than of preserving unity in it. He has more charity for the transgressors of a law than for the observers of it, more for the offence than for the constitution. When the subject says he cannot yield, the Trimmer says the Government must. He takes away the rule that the people may not break it.' The title which had moved the scorn of L'Estrange is cheerfully adopted by the Marquis, whose pamphlet was designed, not only to rebut accusations, but to outline a political programme. A copy was sent to the King, and many passages denote that it was written for the royal eye.

The tract opens with a defence of the offending label. 'This innocent term Trimmer signifieth no more than this, that if men are together in a boat and one part of the company would weigh it down on one side, and another would make it lean as much to the contrary, it happeneth there is a third opinion of those who conceive it would do as well if the boat went even, without endangering the passengers.' The foundation of the Trimmer's faith is a great veneration for laws. 'He looketh upon them as chains that tie up our unruly passions, which else, like wild beasts let loose, would reduce the world into its first state of barbarism.'

Holding laws to be jewels, he believes them to be nowhere better set than in the British Constitution, which, though not perfect, preserves more excellences and fewer faults than any other. Rejecting pure monarchy, which leaves men no liberty, and pure commonwealth, which secures no tranquillity, we have chosen a wise mean. 'We take from one the too great power of doing hurt, from the other the confusion of parity.' It being impossible to hold the balance exactly even, our government leans rather towards monarchy; for a commonwealth requires a higher standard of wisdom and virtue than is to be actually found. Monarchy provides the bells and the tinsel that men love; for the greater part of mankind are and always will be slaves. And when it is in good hands it puts all other forms of government out of countenance.

Though Halifax was sometimes accused of being a secret republican, it is clear that he regarded monarchy as the only possible system for England; but it was a limited monarchy that he advocated. High-strained arguments for the rights of princes provoked human nature. 'When all is said, there is a natural "reason of State"—an undefinable thing, grounded upon the common good of mankind—which is immortal, and in all changes and revolutions preserveth its original right of saving a nation when the letter of the law would destroy it.' Here was a warning, courteous but specific, of the storm that was to break in 1688. 'Our Trimmer', continues Halifax, 'owneth a passion for liberty, yet so restrained that it doth not in the least impair or taint his allegiance. He thinketh it hard for a soul that doth not love liberty ever to raise itself to another world. He taketh it to be the foundation of all virtue and the only seasoning that giveth a

relish to life. Though the laziness of a slavish subjection has its charms for the more gross and earthy
part of mankind, yet to men made of a better sort of
clay all that the world can give without liberty hath
no taste.' After this full-throated paean the writer
returns to the Constitution, in which dominion and
liberty are happily reconciled. 'It giveth to the Prince
the glorious power of commanding freemen, and to the
subjects the satisfaction of seeing that power so lodged
that their liberties are secure. It doth not allow a
ruining power but a cherishing and protecting power.
Though in some instances the King is restrained, yet
nothing in the government can move without him. Our
laws make a true distinction between vassalage and
obedience, between devouring prerogatives and a
licentious freedom.' 'Our Trimmer is a friend to
Parliaments, notwithstanding all their faults and
excesses, which of late have given such matter of
objection to them.' He proceeds to advocate the
immediate summoning of a Parliament, because it is
an essential part of the Constitution, because it is
enjoined by the Triennial Act, and because nothing
else can unite and heal the nation.

Though Halifax was often described as an atheist,
no one could speak with greater emphasis on the value
of religion to the individual and the community.
'Without it man is an abandoned creature, one of the
worst beasts Nature hath produced, fit only for the
society of wolves and bears; therefore in all ages it
hath been the foundation of government. Without its
help the laws would not be able to subdue the perverseness of men's wills, which, like wild beasts,
require a double chain to keep them down.' But his
respect for religion does not exclude some pointed

criticism of the Church. 'Our Trimmer would have
the clergy supported in all their lawful rights; yet he
thinketh that possibly there may be in some of them
a too great eagerness to extend the ecclesiastical
jurisdiction, which is so unlike the apostolic zeal that
the world draweth inferences from it which do the
Church no service.' A second shaft is directed against
its intolerance. 'As it is a sign of a decayed constitution
when Nature with good diet cannot expel noxious
humours without calling foreign drugs to her assistance, so it looketh like want of health in a Church when
it should have a perpetual recourse to the secular
authority.' A third arrow with an even sharper point
is aimed at the clergy 'who wear God's liveries as some
old warders in the Tower do the King's, who do
nothing that belongeth to their place but receiving the
wages of it'.

The Trimmer recommends the toleration of
Nonconformists, with whom, however, he has little
sympathy. 'Even in those who mean well and are
misled, he looketh on it as a disease that hath seized
upon their minds.' With the Catholics he deals in far
greater detail, for it was a subject on which he entertained strong convictions. 'If a man would speak
maliciously of this religion, he might say it is like those
diseases where, as long as one drop of the infection
remaineth, there is still danger of having the whole
mass of blood corrupted by it.' In a brilliant and bitter
passage he expresses his wonder that the Old Lady
Rome, with all her wrinkles, should yet have charms
able to subdue great princes. 'So far from handsome,
yet so imperious; so painted, yet so pretending; after
having abused, deposed and murdered so many of her
overs, she still findeth others glad and proud of their

new chains. She sitteth in her shop and selleth at
dear rates her rattles and her hobby-horses, while the
deluded world still continueth to furnish her with
customers.' It was one of the most disastrous results
of the Civil War that the English princes had been
driven abroad by Protestants and hospitably received
by Catholics. Turning to the question what the
Government should do he advocates a combination of
firmness and mildness. 'Papists we must have among
us; and if their religion keepeth them from bringing
honey to the hive, let the Government try at least by
gentle means to take away the sting from them.' He
appeals to both parties to exercise self-control. 'It is
to be wished that the Protestants might not be so
jealous as still to smell the match that was to have blown
up the King and both Houses; and on the other side
that the Papists may not be led by any hopes to an
ostentation which must provoke men to be less kind to
them.' It was the policy of tolerating Catholicism while
excluding Catholics from office which he advocated
throughout his political life.

The closing section of the pamphlet is devoted to
foreign policy. Owing to the rivalry of France and
Spain, it was our interest to hold the balance between
them; but the equality which we might for ever have
preserved was in an unlucky hour destroyed by
Cromwell's support of the stronger against the weaker
State. The Trimmer has no bias for or against France,
for Spain at her height was no better. He is filled by
the just fear of an overgrown power, since ambition
is a devouring beast. To support France is to strengthen her for a spring upon ourselves. In a famous
passage the cool and reserved Halifax speaks for once
direct from his heart. 'Our Trimmer is far from

idolatry in other things; in one thing only he cometh near it—his country is in some degree his idol. For the earth of England, to him there is divinity in it, and he would rather die than see a spire of English grass trampled down by a foreign trespasser.' The treatise concludes with a pregnant paragraph in which God and nature are summoned to reinforce the gospel of the *juste milieu*. 'Our climate is a Trimmer between that part of the world where men are roasted and the other part where they are frozen. Our Church is a Trimmer between the frenzy of fanatic visions and the lethargic ignorance of Popish dreams. Our laws are Trimmers between the excesses of unbounded power and the extravagance of liberty not enough restrained. True virtue hath ever been thought a Trimmer, and to have its dwelling midway between the two extremes. Even God Almighty Himself is divided between His two great attributes, His mercy and His justice. In each company our Trimmer is not ashamed of his name, and willingly leaveth to the bold champions of either extreme the honour of contending with no less adversaries than nature, religion, liberty, prudence, humanity and common sense.'

This pregnant and eloquent work, packed with thought and observation, is the greatest political pamphlet of the seventeenth century. While Locke was shortly to state the argument for limited monarchy on broad commonsense lines, Halifax steers towards his goal with the aid of wit and raillery, illustration and aphorism. At a moment when the country had been violently split into Whigs and Tories, he protests against the creation of permanently hostile camps. On the one hand rulers are frankly warned that if they go too far they will be swept away. On the

other he calmly ignores the appeal to the Law of
Nature and to a social contract. His warnings fell on
deaf ears. The British monarchy was mortally stricken
in 1688, and its power was further reduced by the first
two Georges. When the Crown ceased to be the real
executive, government by party, against which the
life and writings of the Trimmer were a sustained
protest, became inevitable. He was a keen observer
and a lucid thinker; but he did not possess the gift of
prophecy.

Though Halifax saved the crown for the Duke of
York by defeating the Exclusion Bill, his unconquerable dislike of Catholicism drove him into opposition
during the reign of James II. Despite his attachment
to the principles of toleration, he unhesitatingly
opposed the Declaration of Indulgence, which, in
opening the door to Nonconformists, was designed to
let in the Catholics. Toleration for Catholics was only
possible if they were excluded from office. Among the
first attacks on the Declaration was the *Letter to a
Dissenter*, issued anonymously. Thousands of copies
were instantly sold, and its importance was attested
by the number of replies which it evoked. Its message
was the danger of accepting gifts from Rome. A
momentary relief would be purchased at the cost of the
national liberties. Against the mother of persecution
all Protestants must maintain a common front. 'These
new friends did not make you their choice but their
refuge. The alliance between liberty and infallibility
brings together the two most contrary things in the
world. The Church of Rome doth not only dislike
allowing liberty, but by its principles it cannot do it.
To come so quick from another extreme is such an
unnatural motion that you ought to be on your guard.

The other day you were sons of Belial, now you are angels of light.' To support the dispensing power when it gave toleration was to facilitate the repeal of every law made for the preservation of Protestantism. 'For this pretended liberty of conscience your real freedom is to be sacrificed.' If Protestants held together the danger would pass away like a shower of hail. 'Let us be still, quiet and undivided, firm at the same time to our religion, our loyalty and our laws.' The heir to the throne was Princess Mary, a Protestant. Relief granted by a Protestant ruler would be permanent, by a Catholic a mere move in the game.

A year later, on the eve of the crash, Halifax returned to the charge in a longer pamphlet. The King's proclamation, announcing the summoning of a Parliament, foreshadowed a guarantee of the Established Church as consideration for the repeal of the Test Act and the penal laws. It was this proposed bargain which Halifax attacked in his *Anatomy of an Equivalent*. The pamphlet develops the arguments of the *Letter to a Dissenter* in a less popular form. Indeed, it is rather a treatise than a tract. The unsleeping suspicion of Catholicism is none the less visible. As Rome had taught that no faith need be kept with heretics, Halifax rejoins that no faith can be expected from Rome. 'At the first setting out she maketh herself incapable of dealing upon terms of equality by the power she claimeth of binding and loosing, which hath been so often applied to treaties as well as to sins. There is no bartering with infallibility, it being so much above equality that it cannot bear the indignity of a true equivalent.' To make a contract with such a party is madness, for it cannot be fulfilled. A promise —even the promise of a king—is no security for its execution. 'Where distrusting may provoke anger and trusting may bring ruin, the choice is easy.'

The necessity of a decision was evaded by the expulsion of the Catholic King. Though Halifax had done more than any man to defeat his project of sapping and mining the Protestant fortress, he refused to share the responsibility of making the Revolution. Yet he was more of a Whig than of a Tory, though he felt a mild contempt for both creeds. Entirely lacking devotional sentiment for the Stuarts or reverence for the hereditary principle, he gladly exchanged a Catholic for a Protestant monarch. Moreover, William embodied the policy of the Dutch *entente* which he had advocated throughout life. He quickly learned to admire the King who truthfully declared himself a Trimmer, and who showed his desire to stand above party by appointing the Whig Shrewsbury and the Tory Nottingham to high office. The Marquis himself, who was the chief instrument in defeating the proposal of a Regency, was William's chief counsellor for the first year of his reign. But the King was his own Prime Minister, and in 1690 Halifax withdrew, his master assuring him that he was still a Trimmer and would continue so. Though the Jacobites sounded him and he returned a civil reply, he never did more than coquet with St. Germains. He thought the return of James not impossible, and desired to effect a cheap insurance without incurring disloyalty to his new master or undertaking responsibilities towards the old. During the years preceding his death in 1695 he surveyed affairs from the detached standpoint of an observer.

The great Trimmer occupied the leisure of his closing days in the composition of further political tracts. His brief but pregnant essay, *A Rough Draft of a New Model at Sea*, published in 1694, is of importance for his conception of maritime power. 'To the question, What shall we do to be saved in this world? there is no other answer but this, Look to your moat. The first article of an Englishman's political creed must be that he believeth in the sea; without that there needeth no general council to pronounce him incapable of salvation.' 'We are confined to an island by God Almighty not as a penalty but as a grace, and one of the greatest that can be given to mankind.' For this reason the Navy is of such importance that it would be disparaged by calling it less than the life and soul of the Government. During the last weeks of his life the *Cautions to Electors* once more attacked his old enemy, the party system. Whigs and Tories, Jacobites and Republicans alike feel the sting of his lash. Independent members, with courage to determine questions on their merits, are to be preferred to the zealots. Dandies, drunkards, absentees, pensioners, placemen, carpet-baggers, spendthrifts, bores—these and many other undesirables are passed in review and receive their appropriate chastisement. In advocating some further exclusions the author speaks for himself. He complains of an abuse, 'which daily increaseth, of sending such to Parliament as are scarce old enough to be sent to the University'. If he had his way he would allow no one to become a member under thirty. Lawyers, except those of eminent merit, should not be chosen, and the House is no place for officers. The most characteristic part of the tract is the attack on party. 'I cannot forbear to put in a caveat against men tied to a party. Such a man can hardly be called a free agent, and for that reason is very unfit to be trusted with the people's liberty after he hath given up his own.' 'The heat of a party is like the burning of a fever.' In this as in his other writings he wholly failed to recognize the valuable elements in the party system. After his elaborate review of candidates who ought not to be chosen, he concludes with the advice, 'Choose Englishmen. And when I have said that I will not undertake that they are easy to find.' The tract is mordant and even cynical, and only a Parliament of Halifaxes would have satisfied his fastidious taste.

Long after the death of the Marquis his *Thoughts and Reflections* were issued in 1750; but there is nothing to show whether the collection was arranged by the author. These brilliant aphorisms, the nearest English equivalent to the Maxims of La Rochefoucauld, reveal the personality as well as the opinions of the writer. He thinks poorly of human nature, and his rapier wit flashes round the follies and illusions of men. In the 'Political Thoughts' with which the series opens he scoffs at the shibboleths of controversy. 'Fundamental is used as men use their friends—commend them when they have need of them, and when they fall out, find a hundred objections to them.' On the royal power he is admirably sane. 'If kings are only answerable to God, that doth not secure them even in this world, since if God upon the appeal thinketh fit not to stay, He maketh the people His instruments.' 'Kings assuming prerogative teach the people to do so too.' There are obvious touches of personal experience in the aphorisms on Ministers. 'The world dealeth with Ministers as they do with fiddlers, ready to kick them downstairs for playing ill, though few of the fault-finders understand their music enough to be good judges.' 'It is dangerous to serve where the master hath the privilege not to be blamed.' 'A prince should be asked why he will do a thing, not why he hath done it.'

For the people Halifax feels pity not unmixed with contempt. 'When the people contend for their liberty they seldom get anything by their victory but new masters.' 'The body of the people are generally either so dead that they cannot move or so mad that they cannot be reclaimed. To be neither all in a flame nor quite cold requireth more reason than great numbers can ever attain.' 'As mankind is made, the keeping it in order is an ill-natured office. It is like a great galley, where the officers must be whipping with little intermission.' 'A nation is a mass of dough; it is the Government that kneadeth it into form.' Yet the government is as little to be trusted as the people. 'Power is so apt to be insolent and Liberty to be saucy that they are very seldom upon good terms.' The difficulties of rule have been increased by the appearance of the party system, at which Halifax once more discharges a flight of arrows. 'The best party is but a kind of conspiracy against the rest of the nation.' 'Ignorance maketh most men go into a party, and shame keepeth them from getting out of it.' In this world of disenchantment there are few who are good and still fewer who are wise.

Halifax and Hobbes are beyond comparison the most stimulating political writers of seventeenth-century England. Though they differed fundamentally in their teaching—the one preaching an absolute, the other a limited government—they were alike in finding no party or body of men who shared their views. The main cause of the isolation of Halifax was, of course, his detestation of party; but a further ground was the modernity of his thought. While his contemporaries appealed to fundamental principles and natural law, to Scripture and to precedent, he approached politics in a purely empirical spirit. He tested theories by their working and claims by their fruits. His career showed that he was far more than a mere arm-chair politician, and Macaulay has remarked that his decisions most nearly anticipated the verdict of posterity. Though he never wrote a comprehensive treatise, his pamphlets contain more thought and observation than is to be found in the same space elsewhere in English political literature. His personality impressed everyone with whom he came in contact, whether favourably or otherwise. If the sceptical aristocrat had a fault as a thinker, it was that he scarcely realized the reserves of wisdom and sanity latent in the average unlettered citizen.

CHAPTER X

THE STATE AND RELIGION

I

No problem occupied the minds of political thinkers during the seventeenth century more insistently than that of the relation of the State to religion. While Protestants of every school combined to repudiate the pretensions of the Pope, they disagreed as to the person or body in whom authority over religious belief and practice should be lodged. Luther transferred it to the secular ruler, and his unflinching Erastianism was generally followed by Protestant States. On the other hand, Calvin and his disciples taught that the Church should dominate the State and control the life of its members. Neither at Wittenberg nor at Geneva was any place found for the toleration of minorities. The founders of religious liberty were not the Reformers, but the Unitarians who rebelled against their yoke. The Socinian catechism of Rakau, published in 1605, first enunciated religious liberty as an article of faith among an organized body of Christians. In fighting for their own existence they were fighting for the spiritual liberty of the world. The task of emancipation was continued by Arminius and Episcopius in their crusade against the iron Calvinism of the Netherlands.

In England no notable champion of toleration arose before the seventeenth century. Though More prescribed it for Utopia, his practice was that of his age. The Elizabethan settlement, though designed for comprehension, found no place for small minorities.

More generous ideas filtered in from Holland. In 1582, in his *Life and Manners of all True Christians*, Robert Brown, then resident at Middelburg, issued the first defence by an Englishman of full religious liberty, and denied the magistrate every species of ecclesiastical authority. To the small community of Arminian Baptists who followed their pastor Helwisse to London in 1611 belongs the glory of the first collective declaration of religious liberty in Great Britain. In their *Confession of Faith*, published in 1611, and in the little volume, *Religious Peace, or a Plea for Liberty of Conscience*, published in 1614, the doctrine is clearly stated. Its author, Leonard Busher, was probably a member of Helwisse's congregation. He reminds King and Parliament that the imposition of a belief by fire and sword is utterly contrary to the merciful law of Christ, who wishes not to destroy, but to save the lives of men. Neither King nor bishop can compel belief any more than they can command the wind. As the wind bloweth where it listeth, so does the Spirit of God work with the soul of man. 'I read that Jews, Christians and Turks are tolerated in Constantinople and live together in peace. If this be the case, how much more ought not Christians to keep themselves from restraining other religions? There can be nothing not only more ruthless but more unnatural and abominable than that a Christian should persecute and oppress another Christian."

A few years later a remarkable address was delivered by John Robinson, an Independent minister, at the departure of the *Mayflower*. 'If God reveal anything to you by any other instrument of His, be as ready to receive it as ever you were to receive any truth by my ministry; for I am verily persuaded the Lord has more truth yet to break forth out of His Holy Word. The Lutherans cannot be drawn to go beyond what Luther saw, and the Calvinists stick fast where they were left by that great man of God, who yet saw not all things.' This generous exhortation, perhaps somewhat polished by its reporter, contained one of the earliest statements of the notion that religious truth is progressively revealed, and that sects and Churches must learn from one another. While, however, a few single voices were raised for toleration, the nation at large continued to regard it as both wicked and dangerous. The hatred of Catholicism was revived by Gunpowder Plot, and the anti-Trinitarians, Legatt and Wightman, were burned under James I. None the less a more gentle spirit began to emerge in the Anglican Church. A complete theory of toleration was implicit in Hooker, who taught that reason was of divine origin as well as Scripture, and that ecclesiastical government was mainly a matter of expediency. The High Church movement of the following generation was denounced as Arminianism by suspicious Calvinists; but though Laud was tolerant towards Catholicism he had no mercy for Protestant dissenters.

While Laud and the Puritans were at open war a remarkable school of Anglican thinkers arose, combining broad views of theology with a generous attitude to minorities. The first of these rational theologians was 'the ever-memorable' John Hales. He had been present at the Synod of Dort in 1619, when the Arminians were vanquished by the Calvinist majority; and the fierce struggle left an abiding memory of disgust. In his own words, he bid John Calvin good night, and in his quiet life as Fellow of Eton he felt his way towards a comprehensive type of Christianity, taking from the Arminians the far-reaching distinction between fundamental and non-fundamental doctrines. His tract on Schism, published in 1636, gave offence to Laud, who frightened him into an apology. None the less his writings and impressive personality did much to teach that doctrinal differences ought not to interrupt the unity of the Church. Religion was of God, theology of man. 'Liberty of judging' was a Christian right, truth and error the responsibility of the individual. The spirit was of more importance than the doctrine. 'He thought', wrote his friend Clarendon, 'that other men were more in fault for their carriage towards them than the men themselves who erred, and that pride and passion, more than conscience, were the cause of all separation from each other's communion, and he frequently said that that only kept the world from agreeing upon such a liturgy as might bring them into one communion.' Heresy and schism were two theological scarecrows. Only wilful error could be called heresy. Not only individuals but Councils and Synods had often erred. Clarendon records the dictum that he would renounce the religion of the Church of England to-morrow if it obliged him to believe that any other Christian should be damned. This gentle apostle of toleration, though little known in the market-place, was reverenced by a large circle of friends and scholars, and the Tract on Schism became canonical with the Latitudinarians who were to succeed the Anglo-Catholics in the control of the Church.

Of far greater celebrity than Hales was his friend Chillingworth, who, after a brief sojourn in the Roman Church, launched his famous apologia, *The Religion of Protestants*, in 1637. The devoted friend of Falkland

and perhaps the most brilliant member of the circle at Great Tew, he impressed friend and foe by his dialectical ability. Clarendon warmly praises his great subtlety, incomparable power of reason and his 'rare sharpness and quickness of argument'. In answer to his Jesuit antagonist, he declares that the Bible, and the Bible alone, is the religion of Protestants. The meaning of Scripture and the great principles of religion were clear enough. The issues that separated Christians, at any rate Protestants, were not matters of faith, but of speculation. Certitude could almost invariably be reached by any open mind from Scripture and where it was impossible it was unnecessary. Religious latitude was the logical corollary of the Reformation. The Apostles' Creed was the best because the simplest statement of Christianity. 'Why should men be more rigid than God? Why should any error exclude any man from the Church's communion which will not deprive him of eternal salvation? The way to heaven is not narrower now than Christ left it. God does not and man ought not to require any more than this—to believe the scripture to be God's word, to endeavour to find the true sense of it, and to live according to it.'

No English divine had as yet stated the principle of toleration so boldly. He offers it not as a grudging concession to irreconcilable differences, but as a rule for the life and government of Churches. Religious latitude, far from being merely a compromise, was a good in itself. Deifying our own interpretations and tyrannously enforcing them upon others had been the foundation of all the schisms. 'Take away this persecuting, burning, cursing, damning for not subscribing to the words of men as the words of God. Take away tyranny. Require of Christians only to believe Christ.' From the Anglican he differed in denying to the Church the determination of the nature and boundaries of belief, from the Puritan in throwing over much of what seemed essential. He folds all Christians within his generous embrace. The supremacy of Scripture emancipated men from the rival tyrannies of the Churches. That those whose examination of the Bible led them beyond the Christian fold should also have liberty did not occur to one who accepted its traditional interpretation as axiomatic. It would, moreover, have weakened the force of his reply to the champion of an infallible Church. Assuming the infallibility of the Bible, he cannot be called a rationalist; but he mined the citadel of intolerance by separating intellectual error from moral obliquity, and substituting charity for uniformity as the basis of a Christian Church.

While Hales and Chillingworth only dealt incidentally with the practical question of toleration, the Chrysostom of the English Church raised his voice in an express plea for religious comprehension. Shortly after his ordination Jeremy Taylor attracted the notice of Laud, who made him one of his chaplains and secured for him, though a Cambridge man, a fellowship at Oxford, where he formed a close friendship with Chillingworth. But whereas *The Religion of Protestants* was addressed to Rome, *The Liberty of Prophesying*, published ten years later, was an attempt to pour oil on the troubled waters of English Protestantism. Laud had died on Tower Hill, Anglicanism was overthrown, Presbyterian was arrayed against Independent. The whole land groaned and travailed because zealots insisted that all men should march to heaven by a single road.

Taylor boldly pronounces religious differences to be grounded in the nature of man. The real mischief lay not in divergence of thought, but in narrowness of mind. 'Every opinion is made an article of faith, every article a ground of quarrel, every quarrel makes a faction, every faction is zealous, and all zeal pretends for God. So we think we love not God except we hate our brother, and we have not the virtue of religion unless we persecute all religions but our own.' Christianity was belief in Christ as the Son of God and the Saviour. That was enough for the primitive Church and it was enough for to-day. The Apostles' Creed contained all that was needed. A man might make 'deductions' from it for himself, but he had no right to force them on others. No Church, no Council could add to it, and those who attempted additions were the true authors of heresy and schism. He himself believed episcopacy to have been enjoined by Christ; but he regarded it as belonging to the well-being of the Church, not to its essence. If it was too late to include in one communion all who accepted the Apostles' Creed, it should still be possible to restore peace among the warring sects. His plea is addressed to his own Church as much as to any other, and he scouts the notion that the members of rival bodies are fools and knaves. 'Certainly among all these sects there are very many wise and good men.'

Passing from the discussion of faith to that of heresy, he proves from the New Testament that the term cannot be applied to doubtful speculative propositions, 'nor ever to pious persons'. As faith apart from moral results has no merit, so error is no heresy unless it springs from ambition or some other failing. If a man sees no reason for altering his opinion, it is his duty as well as his right to maintain it. The early Church allowed a wide liberty of interpretation of Scripture. This period was ended by the Nicene Creed, which he refused to place beside that of the Apostles. Council has contradicted Council, Papal infallibility is a delusion, the Fathers differed from each other. Scripture alone is supreme, and it must be interpreted by private judgement. If we fall into error, it is enough that we have tried to avoid it. Inquiry is not a vice, but a duty. Thus Taylor, like Chillingworth, presents the Apostles' Creed as the bond of the Churches, the measure of Christianity and finds room not only for Presbyterian and Independent, but for Papist and Anabaptist. A special chapter on the latter pleads manfully for the toleration of a sect which had few friends. 'To make a way to heaven straighter than God made it, to refuse our charity to those who have the same faith because they have not all our opinions, is impious and schismatical.' This admirable book represents the high-water mark of Anglican toleration. His liberality was doubtless quickened by the fact that his own communion was for a time the Church of a minority; but its real inspiration lay in the sweetness of temper which marks him out in an age of strident controversy and coarse invective. Though he only demands toleration for Christians, there is not a word to exclude those beyond the pale. The only exceptions from his wide charity are the teachers of rebellion and immorality. Such spaciousness of thought met its natural reward in an intolerant age. The captive King read his old chaplain's book with displeasure, and ordered Hammond, another of his divines, to frame a reply. Of his many critics Samuel Rutherford, the fanatical Scottish Presbyterian, was the most violent.

Yet, despite the protests of rival inquisitors, the *Liberty of Prophesying* was not written in vain, and its gentle appeal was heard by those who had not wholly forgotten that Christianity was a religion of charity and love.

In the year of the Restoration, Stillingfleet, the future Bishop of Worcester and antagonist of Locke, published the last latitudinarian plea made by an Anglican clergyman for several decades. The *Irenicon* appeared when ecclesiastical compromises were being freely discussed. The treatise opens with a gloomy picture of the fruits of religious strife and sectarian dogmatism. In the spirit of Hales, Chillingworth and Taylor he declares that for the Church to require more than Christ had done was wholly unwarrantable. 'What possible reason can be assigned why such things should not be sufficient for communion with a Church which are sufficient for eternal salvation? The unity of the Church is a unity of love and affection, not a bare uniformity of practice and opinion.' Had any particular form of government been necessary it would have been revealed by Christ. Even the practice of the Apostles, could we accurately discover it, would not bind future ages, as times and circumstances alter. If the idea of a single exclusive system could be overthrown a compromise would be easy, and Episcopacy and Presbyterianism might be combined. Every communion rightly possessed its own rules; but they must not be mistaken for divine injunctions. He quotes with approval the saying of Ambrose, 'When at Rome I fast on the Sabbath, when at Milan I do not'. He dreams of a Church imposing nothing beyond what is clearly revealed in Scripture. To insist on a multitude of forms and ceremonies was to invite and even to compel schism. Simplification was urgently needed, and a revision of the Liturgy to meet the scruples of the Presbyterians should be taken in hand. Neither Episcopacy nor Presbyterianism could point to a single word of Christ in support of a claim to divine right. By an elaborate study of the apostolic age he shows that the Church adapted itself to local circumstances, and its organization was a human and historic growth, 'a mere matter of prudence'. On the strength of this discovery he appeals for an end 'of our un-Christian animosities, while we pretend to serve the Prince of Peace'.

During the middle decades of the century, the argument for toleration was reinforced by a second group of Churchmen. While Chillingworth and Taylor envisaged theology from the ecclesiastical side, the Cambridge Platonists approached it through the avenue of philosophy. Their reaction against a narrow, traditional dogmatism paved the way for an eclecticism which led straight to toleration. The individual Christian should not only interpret the Bible for himself, but construct his own philosophy of religion. Cudworth declared in a sermon before the House of Commons in 1647 that the object of religion was not to propagate opinions, but to persuade men to the life of Christ. 'The maintenance of truth', declared Whichcote, 'is rather God's charge, the continuance of charity ours.' The lofty aim of the school was to state theology in terms of reason and morality. For this reason, however, their contribution to the defence of toleration was more indirect and less powerful than in the case of those who placed it in the forefront of their argument, and focused attention upon it as a problem of practical statesmanship.

The gospel of religious liberty was expounded from a widely different standpoint by one of the most striking personalities of English Nonconformity. Roger Williams had crossed to America in 1631, but found that life in Massachusetts was not such as he had anticipated. On becoming pastor of Salem he urged his flock to separate from the other Churches of the colony. His attack on the Charter and his contention that the land still belonged to the natives led to his expulsion. His congregation, which followed their pastor to Providence, undertook to obey all laws made by a majority of their number, providing that they dealt exclusively with civil affairs. The principle of liberty of conscience was explicitly affirmed. A second wave of emigrants reached Narragansett Bay, and named their place of settlement Rhode Island. Williams now sailed to England and brought back a charter empowering the settlements to 'rule themselves as they should find most suitable to their condition'. The residents thereupon declared that 'the form of government established is democratical, that is a government held by free consent of all or the greater part of the free inhabitants'. A series of Acts and Orders was then adopted, forming a Declaration of the Rights of Man. Five years later slavery was abolished.

The founder of Rhode Island was not content with establishing a colony of politically and spiritually free men. While still residing in Massachusetts he had sent a copy of an early Baptist plea for liberty of conscience to Cotton, with a request for his opinion on it. Cotton distinguished between fundamentals and circumstantials, and disclaimed persecution for 'conscience rightly informed'. 'But if the heretic persists in his errors after admonition, it would not be out of conscience.' In reply to this doctrine of conditional toleration Williams published *The Bloody Tenet of Persecution*. He boldly rejects the reservation of fundamentals. Whatever such points were reserved, the souls of thousands who did not accept them were 'bound upon the bundle of eternal life'. The civil sword could make a nation of hypocrites, but not a single Christian. Like Robert Brown, the founder of Congregationalism, he asserted that magistrates possessed no ecclesiastical authority. In a word, freedom of thought might not only be granted with safety, but could not be withheld without danger. Sovereignty resided in the people, who might create what form of government they liked. But even they could not give the magistrate religious jurisdiction, since they did not possess it themselves. The Prelatists, Presbyterians, and Independents all aspired to 'sit down under the shadow of that arm of flesh'; but the Separatists alone could make a fair claim to the spirit of Christ. While the Liberal Anglicans desired the comprehension of all Christians in a national Church, Williams cared nothing for the ideal of unity, and encouraged every individual to join or form an autonomous group of worshippers.

His faith in his principles was quickly put to the rough test of experience. A settler who forbade his wife to attend the pastor's ministrations so frequently was disfranchised on the ground that he had broken his oath to respect liberty of conscience. An antinomian arrived whose 'denials of all order' were rewarded by imprisonment. In another case some of the colonists declared it 'blood-guiltiness' to execute judgement on transgressors. Williams replied that the commander must determine the ship's course, and that justice, peace, and sobriety must be kept. The sorest trial came in 1656, when the sister colonies agreed to exclude 'all Quakers, Ranters and notorious heretics', and invited Rhode Island to do the same. The General Assembly replied that freedom of conscience was the foundation of their charter and was prized by them as the greatest happiness men could possess. Massachusetts retorted that the doctrines to which exception was taken tended to 'the absolute overturning of civil government among men'. Advice was thereupon sought from England, whence Commissioners were dispatched. 'Do they live peaceably among you?' it was asked; and when Williams replied in the affirmative they added, 'If they can govern themselves they have no need of your government'. Williams accepted the advice, and Rhode Island remained the home of liberty. It was not without justification that he wrote to Vane, 'We have drunk of the cup of as great liberties as any people under heaven'. Though but a speck on the map, Rhode Island bulks largely as the first place where complete religious liberty was both taught and practised. In England the Commonwealth proved as intolerant as the Monarchy; and Cromwell, though declaring that the State, in choosing men to serve it, takes no notice of their opinions, found it impossible to grant the almost unrestricted latitude which he desired.

II

In the Declaration of Breda, issued on the eve of his restoration, Charles II set a good example to his subjects by the famous words, 'We do declare a liberty to tender consciences, and no man shall be disquieted or called in question for differences of opinion in matters of religion which do not disturb the peace of the kingdom'. He would have approved the historic utterance of Frederick the Great, 'In my kingdom every one can go to heaven in his own fashion'. But he was powerless against Parliament and the Church. The generous Anglicanism of Chillingworth and Taylor had disappeared. The clergy had no wish to make the Savoy Conference a success, and the Act of Uniformity drove two thousand ministers from their parsonages. A declaration of freedom issued by Charles shortly after the great expulsion of 1662 was wrecked by Clarendon and Sheldon. The King needed money, and the Cavalier Parliament only opened its purse in return for permission to pass the vindictive laws collectively known as the Clarendon Code. With the substitution of the Cabal in 1667 a more tolerant spirit entered the Council chamber, Buckingham and Ashley supporting toleration on its merits, and the Catholic Clifford in the hope of alleviating the lot of his friends. In the secret treaty of Dover, concluded in 1670, Charles pronounced himself a Catholic, though he deferred a declaration of his faith. In 1672 the King, supported by his ministers, issued his famous Declaration of Indulgence. 'We declare our will and pleasure that the execution of all penal laws in matters ecclesiastical be immediately and hereby is suspended.' Had it been issued by a monarch whose Protestantism was beyond cavil, the Edict might have met with a different reception. But Gunpowder Plot was still unforgotten, and masses of men were obsessed by the idea of Catholic conspiracies. Sheldon and his clergy at once raised the shrill cry of No Popery, and the Anglican Church was mobilized against the royal policy. The ecclesiastical opposition was reinforced by those who

resisted the claim of the Crown to suspend the laws
of the kingdom. When the House met in 1673 the
King boldly announced that he was resolved to stand
by his Declaration; but the opposition was too strong
for a prince always in desperate need of money. The
Cabal collapsed, the Declaration was withdrawn, the
Test Act was passed, and the Duke of York resigned
his offices. The King had sincerely desired to relieve
the Catholics, and was not sorry that the same stroke
would have struck the fetters from the Noncom-
formists; but he now realized the strength of anti-
Roman feeling, and never again attempted to curb the
flood of intolerance.

Yet the effects of the Declaration could not be
wholly wiped out. During the year of its operation
numerous dissenting congregations were established,
and Nonconformity recovered the ground it had lost
during the Clarendon régime. 'It was the greatest
blow to the Church since the King's restoration',
wrote the Tory Reresby, 'all sectaries repairing
publicly to their meetings, insomuch that all the laws
could never bring them back in due conformity.'
The Catholics looked forward to a Catholic monarch,
and the Protestants were encouraged by the sympathy
of the King and the public exhibition of their numbers.
Unlike the Declaration of Indulgence in 1687, which
was merely a move in James's Catholic campaign, that
of 1672 was a landmark in the history of religious
liberty. Other influences, moreover, were moving in
a similar direction. Influential men like Petty and
Temple pointed to Holland as an object lesson in the
wisdom of toleration. The new spirit of scientific
inquiry found expression in the foundation of the
Royal Society. Despite the passionate rivalries of the

theologians, the age was becoming more secular and more humane. Glanvill's *Vanity of Dogmatizing* was widely read, and Unitarianism began to spread. It was significant of the atmospheric change that the statute for the burning of heretics was repealed by the Cavalier Parliament.

Though theological arguments for persecution were daily losing ground, it was still possible to create belief in the danger of toleration to the peace of the State. This was the chosen weapon of the most active and truculent of the royalist pamphleteers of the Restoration. Roger L'Estrange was rewarded for his sufferings during the Interregnum by his appointment in 1663 to the control of the Press. He signalized his accession to the censorship by the first of a long series of attacks on religious liberty. The Act of Uniformity, he declared, limited actions, not thoughts; for liberty of practice was 'not only unreasonable but utterly inconsistent both with Christianity and public peace'. 'To ask that ye may govern yourselves by your own consciences is the same thing with asking to be no longer governed by the King's laws. Toleration of all opinions is a toleration of all wickedness, and therefore unlawful.' Nonconformists are saddled with the Civil War and the death of the King. 'Toleration of religion is cousin-german to a licence for rebellion.' He does not argue the question whether opinions are true or false, but judges them by their fruits. He condemns religious liberty in the name of the public safety. In later pamphlets he asserts the authority of the State over religion in language which would have satisfied Hobbes. 'When dissent comes to be practical', he adds, 'it is no longer a plea of conscience but a direct conspiracy against the Government.' Why should the

M

Act of Uniformity be torn up? 'They might as well demand a dispensation for rebellion as for schism.'

Of the numerous controversies of the reign of Charles II on the problem of toleration none attracted so much interest as that between Samuel Parker and Andrew Marvell. The son of a Puritan father, Parker joined the winning side on the Restoration, and won the applause of royalist and Anglican circles by his droll mimicry of the Puritans. He became chaplain to Archbishop Sheldon and rose to be Bishop of Oxford. His indisputable ability and vigorous style made him a formidable controversialist, and he was for many years the most redoubtable exponent of intolerant Anglicanism. In 1670 he published *A Discourse of Ecclesiastical Polity, wherein the authority of the civil magistrate over the consciences of subjects in matters of external religion is asserted, the mischiefs and inconveniences of toleration are represented and all pretences on behalf of Liberty of Conscience are fully answered.* He makes a great parade of confuting Hobbes, and boldly maintains that 'when anything is intrinsically evil in a human law, whether civil or ecclesiastical, God is to be obeyed rather than man'. But when he approaches concrete issues the rights of conscience vanish into thin air. 'Do subjects rebel against their sovereign? 'Tis conscience that takes up arms. Do they murder kings? 'Tis under the conduct of conscience. Do they separate from the communion of the Church? 'Tis conscience that is the schismatic. Everything that a man has a mind to is his conscience.' Toleration was anarchy, coercion the price of peace. If the magistrate may control morals, as all admit, he may also control religion. He denounces the absurdity of passing penal laws and mitigating their operation for fear of wounding consciences. Dissent was sedition. 'If the obligation of laws must yield to that of a tender conscience, how impregnable is he that has a mind to disobey against all the commands of his superiors. A weak conscience', he adds in a cynical aphorism, 'is the product of a weak understanding.' Some men are glad to earn the fame of godly men by suffering some little penalty. 'If they dare to murmur', he concludes, 'and their proud stomachs swell against the rebukes of their superiors, then there is no remedy but the rod and correction. They must be chastised out of their peevishness and lashed into obedience.' Even if ecclesiastical jurisdiction were abused it would be less mischievous than liberty of conscience.

This truculent appeal to the secular arm to trample down opposition provoked a temperate reply from John Owen, a lifelong champion of toleration and the greatest of Independent divines. When Parker retorted with a defence of his treatise, Marvell entered the fray with his chief prose work, *The Rehearsal Transposed*, a title borrowed from Buckingham's popular farce. He has little difficulty in showing the inconsistency of a professing Christian immolating conscience before the State. To Parker's complaint that the Dissenters made an unreasonable fuss over the 'two or three symbolical ceremonies' called sacraments Marvell tersely replies, 'It is because a human institution is herein made of equal force to a divine institution that they are aggrieved'. He administers a resounding reproof to the Christian minister for his want of charity. 'Why is it that this kind of clergy should always be for the most precipitate, brutish and sanguinary counsels? The Civil War cannot make them wise nor His Majesty's happy return good-natured. If they would but keep

to their Bibles they might make the best ministers of
State in the world; yet it is generally observed that
kings miscarry under their government. If there be
any counsel more precipitate, more violent, more
extreme than others, it is theirs.' He appeals from
priests to kings, 'who are incumbents of the whole
kingdom and condescend to many things for peace
sake that your proud heart would break before it
would bend to'.

Marvell's book, sparkling with wit and barbed with
satire, won instant popularity. 'Parker', writes Burnet,
'was attacked by the liveliest droll of the age, who writ
in a burlesque strain, but with so peculiar and enter-
taining a conduct that from the King down to the
tradesman his books were read with great pleasure,
and not only humbled Parker but the whole party, for
he had all the men of wit on his side.' When Parker
replied with a volume of bitter personalities, the
member for Hull issued a *Second Part of the Rehearsal
Transposed*. After a scathing exposure of his foe's
self-seeking career, he speaks in impressive tones of
the madness not less than the wickedness of intolerance.
'What prince that sees so many millions of men, either
labouring industriously toward his revenue or adven-
turing their lives in his service, but conceives at the
same time a relenting tenderness over them, whereof
others out of the narrowness of their minds cannot be
capable? Whoever shall cast his eye through the
history of all ages will find that nothing has succeeded
better than the clemency of government. It can
scarcely be reckoned how powerful a magic there is
in a prince who shall go on daily gaining upon the
affections of his people.' While the theologians, Hales,
Chillingworth, and Jeremy Taylor, had attacked

persecution as contrary to the spirit of Christ, Marvell
condemned it as fatal to the strength and unity of the
State.

A far greater and more impressive champion of
toleration was William Penn, whose *Great Case of
Liberty of Conscience once more briefly debated and
defended* was issued in 1671 from Newgate, where the
author was undergoing one of his periodical imprison-
ments. The great Quaker, like other members of his
sect, demanded religious liberty, not because he was
a sufferer, but because it was implicit in the principles
of his communion. To the believer in an inner light
coercion was an outrage. 'The Tower', he declared, 'is
to me the worst argument in the world.' Restraint or
persecution in matters of conscience constituted an
invasion of the Divine Prerogative. Again, the use of
force involved the overthrow of Christianity, for
Christ's kingdom was spiritual. Thirdly, coercion was
contrary to the plain teaching of the Bible. Fourthly,
it was destructive of the natural right to liberty and of
the principle of reason, since we cannot believe against
our understanding. 'Must men be persecuted here if
they do not go against their conscience, and punished
hereafter if they do?' Finally, coercion stirs up resent-
ment and injures the wealth and unity and power of
the country. 'Force never yet made either a good
Christian or a good subject.' The brief but precious
pamphlet ends with a disclaimer of seditious principles,
coupled with the announcement that the Quakers
would continue to meet, whatever the cost.

Four years later, in 1675, Penn repeated his arguments in a second pamphlet, *England's Present Interest
Discovered*. He now emphasized the political and
commercial arguments for toleration, in the hope that

they might strike home where appeals to reason and Scripture had fallen on deaf ears. Persecution damaged trade and discouraged immigration. Moreover, if another State were to offer liberty of conscience, a million Dissenters might leave the country. Holland had risen to greatness by opening her doors. So far from being a defence against anarchy, intolerance was a peril to the government. Not only could it not bring the whole nation into the Church, but it endangered such unity as still existed. Severity led to conspiracy, while toleration would unite all sects in support of the established order. The nation was greater than the Church and should not be sacrificed to it. At the height of the Popish Plot panic in 1679 Penn's *Address to Protestants* reiterated the arguments of his previous pamphlets, and urged that virtue, not opinion, was the cement of society. Like Roger Williams, Penn had the opportunity of applying his principles in the New World. In the constitution with which he presented Pennsylvania in 1682 no religion received official preference, and every variety of monotheistic faith was allowed.

The toleration which he demanded was at last offered by James II. While Halifax rejected the olive branch from suspicion of the King's motives, Penn gratefully accepted it. He knew James, and believed him to be animated by a sincere affection for religious liberty. He was, moreover, wholly free from the prevalent detestation of Catholicism. He knew that Lord Baltimore's colony of Maryland practised complete toleration, while Quakers had suffered from both Anglicans and Puritans in the Old and the New World. In his *Good Advice to the Church of England, Roman Catholic and Protestant Dissenter* he demanded the equality of Churches, and contested the necessity of one predominant religion. That relief came by way of the prerogative was no objection to Penn, who regarded the penal laws as lacking all moral validity, and believed that the Declaration would be followed by legislative repeal. A few months later James made way for William, and the Toleration Act was placed on the Statute Book. Though it excluded Catholics from its scope and only relieved Dissenters on certain conditions from the penal laws, such liberty as it gave was a permanent conquest; for it rested on the assent of Parliament and public opinion, not on the precarious tenure of a royal Declaration. Thus, after many vicissitudes, the end of the century witnessed and registered a definite advance in the field of religious not less than of political freedom.

CHAPTER XI

THE STATE AND TRADE

DURING the seventeenth century the conviction that the Government should actively concern itself with the industry and commerce of the country was as general as the belief that religion was a department of State.

I

With the break-up of feudal and medieval Europe the economic situation underwent a gigantic transformation. The age of discovery led to the growth of foreign and colonial trade, and the bullion from Spanish America produced revolutionary disturbances in the currencies of the Old World. The Reformation contributed to the rise of great States and powerful governments, which needed men and money for their armies; and the period of religious wars was followed by an era in which commercial interests governed foreign policy. The commercial classes became a powerful factor in the State. Statesmen began to realize the political importance of flourishing industries. While agriculture did not appear susceptible of any rapid development, manufactures gave promise alike of a denser population and of indefinite increase of national wealth. Under the fostering care of the State there seemed no limit to the possibilities of trade. Thus economic competition took its place as a factor in the strife of nations, and the accumulation of wealth became the main concern of every government in the west of Europe.

Mercantilism, or the systematic control of production

and exchange by the State, was not so much a creed as an attitude. But certain beliefs were common to the leading mercantilists of all countries, to Bodin and Montchrétien, to Serra and Mun. The greatest practitioner of economic nationalism was Colbert, and its most characteristic achievement was the British Navigation Act of 1651. Statesmen and theorists alike exalted manufactures above agriculture as a source of national wealth, and placed foreign before domestic trade. They were profoundly convinced of the importance of a large store of the precious metals. They believed that a dense population was a source of strength. They were persuaded that by a wise use of the resources of the State the wealth, the power, and the population of a community could be increased. To achieve this purpose every expedient was held legitimate. One industry was favoured, another discouraged, charters were granted and monopolies established. Colonies were estates to be exploited for the benefit of the mother country. States became forcing-houses for the rearing of industries. The world was parcelled out among privileged companies, which watched over the lives and fortunes of their adventurous members. In a word, mercantilism was an instrument in the creation of a Great Power. Economics were merged in politics.

The kernel of the system as it appears in the writings of its English sponsors was the balance of trade. Struck by the fact that money was *sui generis*, always in demand and always available for use, mercantilists desired so to regulate the dealings of their nation with other countries as to attract and retain the largest possible share of the precious metals. Each country should export the utmost quantity of its own manufactures and import only what it absolutely needed, receiving the difference of the values in cash. This difference was known as the balance of trade, and was taken as the test of the utility of each separate branch of commerce. The balance was described as favourable when more money was received than paid. To achieve this result, on which the welfare of the nation was held to depend, the Government was justified in prohibiting the export or import of certain commodities, in offering bounties on certain exports, in imposing duties on such foreign articles as it allowed to enter, and in regulating and even prohibiting the export of the precious metals. Though wealth was rarely stated to consist exclusively of gold and silver, there was a general tendency in popular thought to confuse wealth and money.

The first systematic discussion of the problems of foreign trade began during the reign of James I, when Gerard Malynes, a specialist in the currency, whose advice on mercantile affairs was often sought by the Privy Council, set forth his views in a series of pamphlets. Since in his view exchange implied value for value, the operations of the exchangers appeared to him to defraud the revenue. He therefore pleaded for the regulation of the process by the Government. The fallacy was attacked by Misselden, an experienced man of business who more than once represented the Merchant Adventurers on foreign missions. His *Free Trade, or the Means to make Trade Flourish* discussed the alleged decay of prosperity, which he attributed to the excessive consumption of foreign commodities. When Malynes replied, Misselden retorted with *The Circle of Commerce or the Balance of Trade*, in which he defended the export of bullion on the ground that by re-exporting the commodities thus purchased a still greater treasure would be ultimately secured. This line of argument exactly tallied with that of his friend Mun, whose most celebrated work gave classical expression to the governing ideas of the time.

Thomas Mun, who is sometimes described as the founder of mercantilism, made his fortune in the Levant trade, and, after gaining much experience abroad, was appointed a Director of the East India Company. It was in defence of the Company that he published a *Discourse of Trade from England to the East Indies*, which answered the complaint that by exporting coin it rendered money scarce. When instituted in 1600 the Company obtained leave to export coin or bullion to the value of £30,000, on condition that they should reimport, within six months of the termination of each voyage, a sum equal to that which had been sent abroad. Even this narrowly restricted privilege, however, was bitterly attacked. A far more important treatise, *England's Treasure by Foreign Trade*, probably written about 1630, was printed in 1664, more than twenty years after his death. Often reprinted during the seventeenth and eighteenth centuries, it retained almost canonical authority till it was displaced by *The Wealth of Nations*.

The sub-title of the treatise declares that 'the balance of our foreign trade is the rule of our treasury', and the object is declared to be to exhibit the means by which a kingdom may be enriched. The keynote is clearly struck in the opening pages. 'The ordinary means to increase our wealth and treasure is by foreign trade, wherein we must ever observe this rule—to sell more to strangers yearly than we consume of theirs in value. For that part of our stock which is not returned to us in wares must necessarily be brought home in treasure.' Every effort must therefore be devoted to increase our exports and to decrease our consumption of foreign commodities. Waste land should be used to grow hemp, flax, and other articles which are now imported. We might also diminish our imports if we would lessen our demand for foreign wares in diet and raiment. The vagaries and excesses of fashion might be corrected by adopting the sumptuary laws prevailing in other countries. 'If in our raiment we will be prodigal, let this be done with our own manufactures, where the success of the rich may be the employment of the poor, whose labours, notwithstanding, would be more profitable if they were done to the use of strangers.' We may charge a high price for articles which our neighbours need and which no other country can supply; but those of which we do not possess the monopoly must be sold as cheap as possible. Foreign materials worked up in England for export should be duty-free. Our exports should be carried in our own ships, and our fisheries should be developed. Writing as a Director of the Company, Mun pronounces our trade with the East Indies the most profitable of our commercial activities, not only because we obtain its products cheaply for ourselves, but because we sell the surplus at a high price to our neighbours. This 'may well stir up our utmost endeavours to maintain and enlarge this great and noble business, so much importing the public wealth, strength and happiness'.

A cogent chapter bears the superscription, 'The Exportation of our Moneys in Trade is a means to increase our Treasure'. The bullionist school demanded that the precious metals should never be allowed to leave the country, or at most under severe restrictions. Realizing the prejudices of the multitude, 'who bitterly exclaim when they see any moneys carried out of the realm', Mun proceeds to argue the question in detail. Accepting the bullionist assumption that trade ought to increase the accumulated store of precious metals, he contends that such a result is best obtained by allowing their unrestricted export. 'Money', he declares, 'begets trade, and trade increaseth money. We must first enlarge our trade by bringing in more foreign wares, which, being sent out again, will in due time bring far greater treasure than was originally sent out.' It is with a kingdom as with individuals, who do not lock up their money but turn it into wares, 'whereby they multiply their money, and so by a continual and orderly change of one into the other grow rich; for they that have wares cannot want money'. Cash is not the life of trade, which began with barter and is now largely carried on with credit. Indeed, a plethora of money raises prices, which is good for certain individuals, but contrary to the public welfare, since demand decreases when the price is raised. We must trade with our money as well as with our merchandise. 'If we only behold the husbandman in the seedtime when he casteth away much good corn into the ground, we will rather account him a madman than a husbandman; but when we consider his labours in the harvest, we find the worth of his actions.'

Mun devotes the longest chapter in his book to Malynes's fallacy that the Exchange possessed almost unlimited power. One by one his 'cunning delusions' are examined and refuted. 'I have lived long in Italy, where the greatest banks and bankers in Christendom do trade, yet could I never see nor hear that they were able to rule the price of exchange by confederacy; but the plenty or scarcity of money in the course of trade did always overrule them and made the exchanges to run at high or low rates.' The work of demolition was so effectively performed that the theory disappeared from the field. Another fallacy at which he tilts is that as usury increases trade decreases; and he has little difficulty in proving that the rate of interest rises with good trade and falls with bad. At the end of the book he returns to his contention that foreign trade is the chief source of wealth and treasure; since in domestic trade the gain of one is the loss of another. It is necessary, however, not to depend exclusively thereon, since if in time of war foreign States prohibit the introduction of English cloth or other commodities, many of our workers would lose their employment. It is therefore essential that tillage and fishing should be undertaken as a supplement to manufactures. 'Yet foreign trade', he concludes, in a strain of eloquent enthusiasm, 'is the great revenue of the King, the honour of the kingdom, the noble profession of the merchant, the school of our arts, the supply of our wants, the employment of our poor, the improvement of our lands, the nursery of our mariners, the walls of the kingdom, the means of our treasure, the sinews of our wars, the terror of our enemies.'

Mun's pamphlet presented the first systematic account of the theory of the balance of trade and how it was to be obtained. Terse in form, lucid in argument, enriched from the stores of a long experience at home and abroad, it triumphantly achieved its immediate purpose of repulsing the attack on the East India Company. The rise of Holland and the decline of Spain provided him with eloquent object-lessons. The publication of his book in 1664, and the simultaneous

permission granted by Parliament to export an unlimited quantity of bullion after entering the amount
at the Custom House, mark the end of the earlier and
narrower variety of mercantilist doctrine which may
be described as bullionism. Mercantilism, as expounded by Mun, was adapted to its time. Though
its theory of the balance of trade was erroneous, it
recognized that the development of industry was the
road to national prosperity. The Navigation Act,
which confined the carrying trade to British vessels or
to those belonging to the country of origin, was a
hindrance to commerce; but it struck a damaging blow
at the Dutch and founded the British mercantile
marine. The practical faults of the system were that
a regulated industry is ill-adapted to changes, and that
trade was sometimes forced into artificial channels. Its
fundamental fallacy was that the commercial advantage
of one country was only to be obtained at the expense
of another.

II

Though mercantilism dominated the theory and
practice of the century, a small group of economists
laid stress during its closing decades on the value of
unrestricted trade. It was something more than a
coincidence that the forerunners of Adam Smith were
Tories. The Whig Party, which owed its origin in
part to hatred of French influence, desired to restrict
trade with that country within the narrowest possible
limits. Thus they conjured up the spectre of over-
balance, buttressing their political animosities by
economic reasoning. The Tories, on the other hand,
who in general supported the Stuart policy of close
relations with France, preached the blessings of open

commerce, and rejected the doctrine of the balance. Charles II naturally approved the French trade, since it provided a substantial and independent revenue. Thus economic theory became the battlefield of political factions. The commercial classes complained that France would grow rich and England poor, and the Whigs, who represented them, declared that 'the wealth of the nation hath been much exhausted by the importation of French commodities'. In 1678 Parliament prohibited the import of French wines, silk, and other articles which were mainly paid for in cash. But the Great Prohibition, as the Act was described, was repealed under James II, and a high tariff was substituted. Imports began to pour in, and when the Revolution overthrew the Tories, the prohibition of all trade with France was renewed. It was now, however, presented and accepted as a war measure. All but Jacobites were eager to weaken France, even if not convinced of the economic wisdom of prohibition.

While the fortunes of parties ebbed and flowed, renewed attempts were made to discuss the problems of commerce in systematic form. The most remarkable of the Tory Free Traders was Dudley North, who, after spending twenty years as a merchant in Smyrna and Constantinople, returned home at the crisis of the struggle between Charles II and the Whigs, and, as Sheriff of London, took a leading part in supporting the royal authority. His incursion into politics was brief, and his fame rests on the *Discourses on Trade*, published in 1691, which Roscher declares might have formed a chapter of *The Wealth of Nations*. A few vigorous strokes shatter the case for the prohibition of trade with France. 'The world as to trade is but as one nation, and nations are but as persons. No trade is unprofitable to the public; for if any prove so, men leave it off; and wherever the traders thrive the public thrives also.' Though Mun had compared the trade of the world to the body, with its members 'accommodating one another', he had not grasped whither his maxims led. With North we breathe a more modern atmosphere. Wealth, he teaches, may exist independently of gold and silver, since it arises from human industry applied to the soil and to manufactures. 'Money is a merchandise, whereof there may be a glut as well as a scarcity, and that even to an inconvenience.' Stagnation of trade is due not to want of money but to overproduction, or to political disturbances at home or abroad. 'All favour to one trade or interest is an abuse, and cuts so much of profit from the public. To force men to deal in any prescribed manner may profit some, but the public gains not, because it is taking from one subject to give to another. No laws can set prices in trade, the rates of which must and will make themselves.' No country can be made rich by State regulations, and the less the Government meddles with trade the better. He makes no attempt to conceal his contempt for sumptuary laws. He directs attention to the importance of the home market, which mercantilists usually overlooked. Finally, he shows that interest depends on supply and demand, and therefore cannot be settled by decree. North's message was that the power of the State to help trade was grossly exaggerated, and that a people only grows rich through peace, industry, and freedom; but his pamphlet quickly disappeared from circulation and was perhaps suppressed.

Similar doctrine is found in the writings of Charles Davenant, a member of Parliament and commissioner

N

of excise, the son of the poet, whose pamphlets appeared in the years immediately following the Revolution. 'Trade', he declares, 'is in its nature free, finds its own channel and best directeth its own course.' He recognized that loss by balance in one trade may cause profit in another. He condemns the study of a single wheel, without regard to the motion of the whole engine. Yet even he blames the Norway and Baltic trade, 'which have always drained us of money'. A third critic of orthodox mercantilism was Josiah Child, for many years the soul of the East India Company, and one of the founders of its greatness. His *Observations on Trade*, published in 1668, reissued and enlarged in 1690 as *New Discourses on Trade*, sharply attacked the theory of the balance. The value of industry was to be measured not by the comparison of imports and exports, but in relation to the trade of the kingdom, by observation of the state of shipping and the patent phenomena of prosperity or decline. He therefore urged commercial freedom and desired to abolish nearly all restrictions on internal industry. Yet he shared more than one of the fundamental convictions of the advocates of restraint, desiring to confine colonial trade to the mother country and discouraging imports which were paid for in cash. He also entertained the curious delusion that the Dutch had stolen our trade owing to the low rate of interest they charged, and maintained that it should be limited by statute to 4 per cent. The fourth member of the Tory Free Trade group, Nicholas Barbon, has only recently won the place that he deserves by the discovery of the authorship of pamphlets hitherto attributed to other writers. His first tract on commerce, published in 1690, denounced 'Prohibitions' as a leading cause of

the decay of trade. If imports really hindered production and consumption of domestic articles, duties
might be imposed to prevent underselling; but such
cases would be very rare. His chief argument against
the balance is the extreme difficulty of discovering it
with accuracy. Moreover, he saw that in the long
run goods paid for goods; and to have grasped that
truth was to have escaped from the toils of mercantilism.

These writers were rather eclectics than Free
Traders, axioms of the old faith jostling anticipations
of Hume and Adam Smith. Yet compared with Locke,
whose economic writings are purely mercantilist, they
are harbingers of a more enlightened generation. They
rejected the notion that national wealth depended on
the accumulation of cash, and established its real
source in nature and labour. They reduced the
exaggerated estimate of foreign commerce, and
emphasized the importance of agriculture. The object
of the State, they proclaimed, was not to secure a
balance of trade, but to obtain for the whole population
the necessities of life. They deprecated the elaborate
system of prohibitions, duties, bounties, and monopolies as an impediment rather than an encouragement
to trade. Their ambition, if not their achievement,
was to take British commerce out of its swaddling
clothes.

III

While most of the economists of the seventeenth
century concentrated their attention on the problems
of external trade, Sir William Petty, the most celebrated of them all, allowed his acute intellect to play
round a variety of subjects of economic and statistical
interest. Obtaining most of his education in France

and Holland, he early formed the acquaintance of men of many countries and pursuits, including the circle which Mersenne gathered round him at Paris. Returning to England in 1646 at the age of twenty-three, he devoted himself for a short time to his father's business as a clothier; but he soon moved to Oxford, where he continued his medical studies. His interest in science and his talent for invention made him one of the leading figures of the scholarly group from which the Royal Society was one day to emerge. His many-sidedness is suggested by the fact that he was at the same time Professor of Anatomy at Oxford and Professor of Music at Gresham College. At no time a keen politician, he was on good terms with men of different parties. Wishing to divide the estates of Irish rebels among the Army and other supporters or creditors of the Commonwealth, the Government employed him to survey the country. The Down Survey of forfeited estates, so called because set 'down' on maps, was the first comprehensive and scientific record of a country. After mapping the lands in question he organized their distribution, and invested his pay in the purchase of land in Kerry. He became private secretary to Henry Cromwell, and after the fall of the Protectorate attended the debates of the Rota Club. Despite his Cromwellian associations, he was welcomed by Charles II, who delighted in the society of scientific men. An original member of the Royal Society, he was knighted in 1662, and contributed several papers on mechanics and inventions to the Transactions. In religion he was a latitudinarian, if not a sceptic. His ambition was to be the head of a new statistical office, which should carry out a census, value the property of the country, reorganize the collection of taxes, and improve the public health. His competence for such a post was universally recognized. 'There was not in the whole world', writes Evelyn, 'his equal for a superintendent of manufactures and improvement of trade. There is nothing difficult to him. If I were a prince, I should make him my second counsellor at least.'

Though Petty was never employed by the Restoration Governments, he composed a considerable number of tracts for the times. The *Observations on the Bills of Mortality of the City of London*, published in 1662, though later attributed to him by Aubrey, Evelyn, and Burnet, were written by his friend Captain Graunt, a clothier who had taken to soldiering in the Civil War, and was now a member of the Common Council. But he may well have aided in its composition, and he edited the work with additions after the author's death. Graunt's volume is of importance as the first scientific attempt at vital statistics. He classifies diseases, studies the age of the victims, and recognizes the evil influence of overcrowding. He discovered the regularity of certain social phenomena, such as the excess of male births, the high mortality of infants, the excess of the urban over the rural death-rate. Nothing so careful and systematic was to appear till the famous treatise of Süssmilch in the following century. Petty described the *Observations* as 'a new light to the world', and he continued his friend's work twenty years later by a treatise on the Dublin returns of mortality. Graunt and Petty rank as the founders of vital statistics, and the impetus they gave to the collection and analysis of sociological data may be traced in the writings of Davenant and Gregory King.

The earliest and most important of Petty's economic writings was his *Treatise on Taxes and Contributions*, published in 1662. This interesting and comprehensive treatise has been described as the most valuable contribution to economic literature before Hume. It was also a programme of national reform, and a plea for the development of the resources of the country. Suggested by the changes in the revenue effected or discussed at the Restoration, his survey covers the different imposts and comments on their character. New burdens were imposed in place of the feudal duties on land then finally abolished, indirect taxation thus largely taking the place of direct. He enumerates the legitimate charges of a State as defence, the maintenance of the Court and administration, the salary of the clergy, the encouragement of education, the maintenance of the poor, the improvement of roads and harbours. After analysing the causes of the unpopularity of the taxes, he turns to possible economies. The revenue of the clergy, whom he loved as little as his friend Hobbes, should be reduced and redistributed, and an army of unnecessary officials should be discharged. The State should find work for the unemployed, and road communications should be greatly improved. In the tract, *Verbum Sapienti*, published in 1664 during the Dutch War, which may be regarded as an appendix to the *Treatise on Taxes*, he drew attention to the over-taxation of land and the under-taxation of the City of London.

Here as elsewhere Petty insists on the necessity of a statistical survey and valuation of land as a basis for a just system of taxation. Passing to Customs and Excise. he reaches the controversial territory over which his brother economists delighted to roam. He establishes the sheer impossibility of prohibiting the export of money, and proves that to prohibit the export of wool and other commodities is equally foolish. 'Suppose', he asks, 'the Hollanders outdo us by more art, were it not better to draw over a number of their choice workmen or send our most ingenious men thither to learn?' In like manner he protests against the prohibition of imports. Let us take away burdensome, frivolous, and antiquated impositions and offices instead of trying to teach water to rise above the level of its spring. 'Labour', he declared in words which quickly became proverbial, 'is the father and active principle of wealth, lands are the mother.' Though he threw over the doctrine of the balance and fully realized that the precious metals were only the tokens of wealth, Petty, like all his contemporaries except Dudley North, stands with one foot in the mercantilist era. He will allow the prohibition of imports if they greatly exceed our exports. Again, he would be ready to forbid the export of wool to Holland if the Dutch lead in the manufacture of cloth were so small that such a step would turn the scale in our favour. It is difficult to be sure whether such men as Petty were aware of their inconsistencies. They may have felt doubtful of their own reasoning, or perhaps they preferred an indirect attack on the mercantilist position.

One of the most original parts of the *Treatise on Taxes* discusses the possibility of finding a standard of value. The worth of gold and silver, he points out, may vary with the supply and other circumstances, and is therefore no absolute standard. To discover such a standard he turns to the cost of production, measured in 'the easiest gotten food of the respective countries'.

The attempt was laudable, but the result highly indefinite. Another interesting section discusses the nature of rent, which he treats as a kind of profit resulting when the expenses of cultivation have been paid. A wise and weighty passage protests against the imposition of penalties as a source of revenue, which leads to an emphatic demand for religious toleration from the point of view of the economist and the statesman. Fines should only be imposed for actual breaches of the peace. To persecute is to damage the State and depress the revenue as well as to afflict the individual. The volume, indeed, is filled with the author's observations on every aspect of policy, and it is as much a handbook for princes as a dissertation on finance.

The most interesting of Petty's later works was the *Political Arithmetic*, which, written when the influence of France had become predominant at Whitehall, was held back till the Revolution made such outspoken criticism free from danger. Instead of using words and arguments, he declares, he has expressed himself in terms of number, weight, or measure. He repudiates the notion that the country is in a decline, and maintains that it has grown in power and wealth for forty years. He endeavours to prove that England's craven policy was not due to weakness, especially if she allied with Holland and copied her commercial policy. 'A small country and few people may by their situation, trade and policy be equivalent in wealth and strength to a far greater people and territory.' That the French Court was more brilliant than the English pointed rather to exploitation than to superior wealth. France is a warning while Holland is a model. The obstacles to England's greatness arose from unwise policy and are removable by a change. The pamphlet breathes a healthy optimism and a vigorous belief in the power and prosperity of the country. Among his minor works were a tract on a project of recoinage, essays on the growth of London, housing and hospitals, and other concrete problems. *The Political Anatomy of Ireland* and the later *Treatise of Ireland* were at once essays in descriptive sociology and attempts at constructive statesmanship. He lamented the subordination of Irish to English interests, and urged an Union to prevent the utter destruction of Irish industries and to allow free commercial intercourse. Political Arithmetic, to use his favourite term, was rather a practical art than a theoretical science. He belonged to the inductive school of political economy. Though a friend of Hobbes, he enlisted under the banner of Bacon. His method was to collect and classify facts, and then to establish some general proposition. Political economy was a branch of statecraft, an attempt to improve the machinery of government and administration. The century which opened with the bullionists and closed with North and Petty cannot be convicted of stagnation.

BIBLIOGRAPHY

[*This bibliography, revised by the author in 1945, includes a number of books published after the original edition of the present work.*]

GENERAL.—G. Davies, *Bibliography of British History, 1603–1714*; Gierke, *The Development of Political Theory*; Meinecke, *Die Idee der Staatsärson*; J. W. Allen, *English Political Thought (1603–1644)*; Gooch and Laski, *English Democratic Ideas in the Seventeenth Century*; Laski, *The Rise of European Liberalism*; A. J. Carlyle, *Modern Liberty*; Dunning, *Political Theories from Luther to Montesquieu*; J. W. Gough, *The Social Contract*; A. Gross, *Der Streit um das Widerstandsrecht*; Hearnshaw (editor), *Social and Political Ideas of the Sixteenth and Seventeenth Centuries*; Maitland, *Collected Papers*, vol. 1; G. N. Clark, *The Seventeenth Century*; G. Davies, *The Early Stuarts*; Gardiner, *History of England, 1603–1656*; Ranke, *History of England, principally in the Seventeenth Century*; McIlwain, *The High Court of Parliament*; Keith Feiling, *History of the Tory Party, 1640–1714*; Holdsworth, *History of English Law*, vols. 4–7; *Cambridge History of English Literature*, vols. 7–8; *Cambridge Modern History*, vols. 4, 5, and 6 (ch. 23); Tröltsch, *Protestantism and Progress*; A. D. Lindsay, *The Modern Democratic State*, vol. 1; Zera Fink, *The Classical Republicans*.

CHAPTER I.—Figgis, *The Divine Right of Kings*; McIlwain, *The Political Works of James I*; Spedding, *Life and Letters of Francis Bacon*;

Abbot, *Francis Bacon*; Church, *Bacon*; Reynold's edition of Bacon's *Essays*.

CHAPTER II.—J. Laird, *Hobbes*; Croom Robertson, *Hobbes*; Tönnies, *Hobbes* (ed. of 1912); Leslie Stephen, *Hobbes*; L. Strauss, *The Political Philosophy of Hobbes*; C. E. Vaughan, *Studies in the History of Political Philosophy*, vol. 1; Gooch, *Hobbes* (Master Mind Lecture at the British Academy, 1940, reprinted in *Studies in Diplomacy and Statecraft*).

CHAPTER III.—'Coke', in *Dictionary of National Biography*; Holdsworth, *Some Makers of English Law*; Holdsworth, 'The Influence of Coke', in *Essays in Legal History*, ed. Vinogradoff; Forster, *Sir John Eliot*; Grosart's Introduction to Eliot's *The Monarchy of Man*; Reynolds' edition of Selden's *Table Talk*; Herbert Paul, *Men and Letters*; *Great Jurists of the World*, ed. Sir John Macdonell.

CHAPTER IV.—Firth, *Oliver Cromwell*; Firth, *Cromwell's Army*; Firth's Introduction to *The Clarke Papers*; Firth's Introduction to Ludlow's *Memoirs*; Gardiner, *Oliver Cromwell*; T. C. Pease, *The Leveller Movement*; T. H. Green, *Four Lectures on the English Commonwealth*; Borgeaud, *The Rise of Modern Democracy*; W. Rothschild, *Der Gedanke der geschriebenen Verfassung in der englischen Revolution*; A. P. Wodehouse, Introduction to *Puritanism and Liberty*; W. Haller, *The Rise of Puritanism*; W. K. Jordan, *Men of Substance*: *Henry Parker and Henry Robinson*; Don M. Wolfe, *Milton in the Puritan Revolution*; Wolfe, *Leveller Manifestos of the Puritan Revolution*.

CHAPTER V.—Masson, *Life of John Milton*; Mark Pattison, *Milton*; Seeley, 'Milton's Political Opinions', in *Lectures and Essays*; Dowden, *Puritan and Anglican*; Liljegren, *James Harrington's 'Oceana'*; H. F. Russell Smith, *Harrington and his 'Oceana'*.

CHAPTER VI.—Petegorsky, *Left Wing Democracy in the Civil War*; Berens, *The Digger Movement*; E. Bernstein, *Cromwell and Communism*; M. Beer, *History of British Socialism*.

CHAPTER VII.—W. A. Shaw, *History of the English Church, 1640–1660*, 2 vols.; Weingarten, *Die Revolutionskirchen Englands*; Tröltsch, *The Social Teaching of the Christian Churches*, vol. 2; Burrage, *The Early English Dissenters*; Dexter, *The Congregationalism of the last Three Hundred Years*; Rufus Jones, *Mysticism and Democracy in the English Commonwealth*; Rufus Jones, *Spiritual Reformers in the Sixteenth and Seventeenth Centuries*; Rufus Jones, *George Fox*; Braithwaite, *The Beginnings of Quakerism*; Braithwaite, *The Second Period of Quakerism*; M. Brailsford, *The Making of William Penn*; M. Brailsford, *James Naylor*; Best, *Rebel Saints*; Kirby, *Prynne*; F. J. Powicke, *Richard Baxter*; Louise F. Brown, *The Political Activities of the Baptists and Fifth Monarchy Men during the Interregnum*; Barclay, *The Inner Life of the Religious Societies of the Commonwealth*.

CHAPTER VIII.—G. N. Clark, *The Later Stuarts, 1660–1714*; Ogg, *England in the Reign of Charles II*; Airy, *Charles II*; Macaulay, *History of England*; Kent, *The Early History of Toryism*; R. C. Christie, *Life of the First Earl of Shaftesbury*;

Louise F. Brown, *The First Earl of Shaftesbury*; Ewald, *Life of Algernon Sidney*; Clarke and Foxcroft, *Life of Bishop Burnet*; Kitchin, *Sir Roger L'Estrange*; Saintsbury, *Dryden*; R. C. Christie, 'Memoir of Dryden', in Globe Edition of his *Poems*; G. M. Trevelyan, *The English Revolution, 1688–9*.

Chapter IX.—Foxcroft, *Life and Letters of Sir George Savile, Marquis of Halifax*; Sir W. Raleigh, Introduction to the Works of Halifax; Herbert Paul, *Men and Letters*.

Chapter X.—Tulloch, *Rational Theology in the Seventeenth Century*; W. K. Jordan, *The Development of Religious Toleration in England*, 4 vols.; M. Freund, *Die Idee der Toleranz im England der grossen Revolution*; Lyon, *The Theory of Religious Liberty in England, 1603–1639*; Seaton, *The Theory of Toleration under the Later Stuarts*; Ruffini, *Religious Liberty*; Bury, *History of Freedom of Thought*; Belasco, *Authority in Church and State*; E. Gosse, *Jeremy Taylor*; Bate, *The Declaration of Indulgence*; Whiting, *Studies in English Puritanism, 1660–1688*; *Cambridge Modern History*, V, chs. 11 and 24; W. Hazard, *La Crise de la conscience Européenne, 1680–1715*, 3 vols.

Chapter XI.—Lipson, *Economic History of England*, vols. 2–3; Cunningham, *The Growth of English Industry and Commerce*; Tawney, *Religion and the Rise of Capitalism*; Hecksher, *Mercantilism*; Schmoller, *Mercantilism*; Ingram, *History of Political Economy*; Palgrave, *Dictionary of Political Economy*; E. A. Johnson, *Early British Economists*; Hewins, *English Trade and Finance chiefly in the Seventeenth Century*; Fitzmaurice, *Life of Sir*

William Petty; *The Economic Writings of Sir W. Petty*, ed. Hull; Mun, *England's Treasure by Foreign Trade*, ed. Ashley; Ashley, 'The Tory Origin of Free Trade', in *Surveys, Historic and Economic*; Roscher, *Zur Geschichte der englischen Volkswirtschaftlehre* (Abhandungen der Sächsischen Akademie, 1867); R. K. Merton, *Science, Technology and Society in Seventeenth Century England* (*Osiris*, Vol. IV, part 2).

INDEX

Printed in Great Britain by The Camelot Press Ltd., London and Southampton